May Daddy God continue to use you to reach out to others with His love always

With love and blessings,
Esther
xx

How a Single Woman Can Overcome Stigmatisation

Thriving in a World of Negative Stereotypes

Esther Kuganja

authorHOUSE®

AuthorHouse™ UK
1663 Liberty Drive
Bloomington, IN 47403 USA
www.authorhouse.co.uk
Phone: 0800.197.4150

© 2017 Esther Kuganja. All rights reserved.

No part of this book may be reproduced, stored in a retrieval system, or transmitted by any means without the written permission of the author.

Scriptures taken from:

The New King James Version®. Copyright © 1982 by Thomas Nelson. Used by permission. All rights reserved.

The Message. Copyright © 1993, 1994, 1995, 1996, 2000, 2001, 2002. Used by permission of NavPress Publishing Group.

Published by AuthorHouse 04/13/2017

ISBN: 978-1-5246-7970-5 (sc)
ISBN: 978-1-5246-7971-2 (e)

Print information available on the last page.

Any people depicted in stock imagery provided by Thinkstock are models, and such images are being used for illustrative purposes only.
Certain stock imagery © Thinkstock.

This book is printed on acid-free paper.

Because of the dynamic nature of the Internet, any web addresses or links contained in this book may have changed since publication and may no longer be valid. The views expressed in this work are solely those of the author and do not necessarily reflect the views of the publisher, and the publisher hereby disclaims any responsibility for them.

What others are saying about this book:
How a Single Woman Can Overcome Stigmatisation

Esther Kuganja has written a deeply passionate, courageous and practical book borne of solid experience and astute personal insight. She describes the single life with an expert 'African voice'. However, many will recognise their own journey in these pages regardless of culture or context.

Whether you are single and wonder if anyone truly understands the challenges you face or you are married and in need of fresh insights into the realities of the single life, look no further than this book. You will be challenged, encouraged and inspired regardless of your marital status. This book will bless you, not simply because it is full of wise 'nuggets' but also because in the words of John 8:32; 'the truth will set you free'.

Rev Dr Kate Coleman
Founder and co-director of Next Leadership
Birmingham, UK.

It's easy to review a book but not this type, as you struggle with the realities of the writer and how they affect your own personal experiences. Esther has taken time to demystify the concept of late singleness and given credibility to the whole essence of humanity. She has dared the devil in many cultures and Christian circles by writing on such a topic as this yet, for a just cause - a cause to restore pride to being single and the virtue of celibacy.

Would people have done this some decades back, there may have been illumination in the African communities and churches. I want to urge every reader to do an active reading and the exercises after each chapter of this book, it may be your turning point and those out there stigmatized. It is worth reading, and should be used as a reference point to developing schemes, in order to change the perception of people towards the problem of stereotyping singles. Happy reading!

Adebayo Samuel Adedoyin,
Lecturer, International Black Sea University,
Georgia.

This is a book written with passion by an African single lady. Based on her experiences and those of her friends, it seeks both to inform and to initiate change. Having become a Christian early in life, the author was forced to contend with poor role models both in the home and the African Initiated Church (AIC). The latter propounded doctrines so far from biblical truths that hurt and anguish were the results, especially amongst single women. These women were led to believe that their singleness was of their own making, that they were at least neglectful and at worst evil. To tackle an issue as deeply ingrained in African culture, where women are regarded as inherently inferior, is brave. To set up an NGO with the aim of raising African leaders of integrity demonstrates an amazing determination to change the status quo. The author vividly describes the transformation she went through, taking her from a depressed female wanting nothing more than a husband, to a self-confident woman able to accept whatever life may bring and to try her utmost to make things better for others, especially single African people.

My emotions whilst reading the book ranged from pity and disbelief, through anger, to admiration and a sense of hope. African Christians will be greatly encouraged and inspired by reading this, and I would dare to hope that African Church leaders, and even African parents, would read it and repent. My prayer first and foremost is that the author will find continued fulfilment and great happiness in life, and secondly that she will see her dreams beginning to materialise in the incredible and beautiful country of her birth.

Julia Margaret Fry,
Retired Teacher,
Warwick, UK.

This is a brilliant memoir of a single woman grasping with the realities of deep gender stereotypes and cultural bias within an African culture, set in the diaspora. I could hardly put the book down, caught in the drama of a young woman grappling with the challenges of purpose, destiny and emotional fulfilment in a world set by cultural bias, religious dogma and societal prejudice. For women in most cultures, having children is a core fulfilment of life, an end in itself and their purpose of existence. How then must a single woman cope? How does the home in which a young girl grows affect her confidence and self-esteem? How do deep childhood and psychological trauma affect how she relates to men? What role does tribalism play?

The book communicates the emotional anguish and the deep struggle of faith, a life enslaved by dogma entrenched teachings. "How do I find love," says the lady? "Will I have a fulfilled life?" "Is marriage the end?" Deep questions plague the human story. But should not the modern society have conquered this? Can a woman not find true purpose outside marriage and children? This book brings hope to many women. She alone must determine her course. She alone must decide her happiness. She must decide what directs her fulfilment. She must transform her understanding and find a purpose bigger than herself. In the end, this is the real issue and the book does bring truth and justice. . Excruciating is the experience single women face but at the same time, very enlightening, inspiring and full of hope.

> **Pastor Olurotimi O. Adeniyi**
> **Founding Director - Institute for Economics and Technology Advancement,**
> **Dean - History Makers Bible School UK,**
> **Managing Partner & Principal Consultant IMS**
> **London, UK**

This book is a great read for anyone who is single particularly if you are from an African or religious background. In many African communities it is not the case that individuals are unaware of the issues and challenges both men and women face on a daily basis, but that these challenges are mostly being discussed as an "undercover". This book is a breath of fresh air and an excellent example of what an individual can do to help many in the community experiencing the same issues.

What the writer expresses may not be new to some of you, but what the book does is to cast more light on what you may already know about being single; it gives the reader support and reassurance that they are not alone. The book encourages the reader not to give up, not to allow people's labels to define who they are. It offers the reader better understanding and easy-to-follow guidelines to help you on your life's journey as a single woman.

> *Winfred Kitaka,*
> *Author, Speaker and Founder of Empowering Mothers LTD,*
> *London, UK.*

Dedication

With great joy, I dedicate this book to all the
single ladies who have patiently endured
all sorts of stigmatisation. You are stars!
To my parents, Mr. and Mrs. Joseph and Emily
Balikuddembe - for their understanding and support.
Last but not least, to my first love, the Lord
Jesus Christ. You are my all in all.

Acknowledgments

This project has been a joint effort of various people:

My gratitude goes to Dr. Sunday Adelaja for being a great teacher and mentor to me. Your books and teachings have grown me in faith, character and leadership. Thank you for inspiring me to write this book.

To Samuel, my best friend and companion - the one who has appreciated my uniqueness. Thanks for your guidance, support and sacrificial giving of your resources to make this project a success. You are a treasure!

Thanks to Julia and Malcolm Fry, for your friendship and for taking time to proofread my work.

I would like to extend my sincerest thanks and appreciation to the people who took time to write an endorsement for this book. Thank you for valuing this work.

To all my family and friends, thank you for your encouragement. God bless you!

Foreword

First of all, I want to commend Esther by saying probably your book is the first of its kind in the whole wide world. I have personally written a book similar to this called *'The Advantages of a Single Lady'*, but it is in Russian, not yet in English. But your book is just absolutely miraculous and mind blowing. The question of stigmatization and stereotypes is just all too common and widespread in our world today. However, concerning the stigmatization that goes with single ladies, it has simply become common place. Unfortunately, the world is used to being quiet on this question. So, to raise this question and write so explicitly on it, is a total deliverance for a countless number of women.

I want everybody who will have the opportunity to lay their hands on this book to do everything possible to promote the book to every single woman. More so, I think this book goes beyond the topic of ladies' singleness. It goes to address all forms of stigmatization, either it's based on color, height, size, social status, career choice, etc. Whatever the case, this is a topic that must be read by all; both men and women married or single.

Esther Kuganja, welcome to a new world for yourself because, after this book, you are going to be in high demand. I will like to propose for you to begin by starting a Facebook page or a blog on the topic of this book.

Esther Kuganja

As the case may be, the whole world is waiting for you Esther.

Blessings.

Pastor Sunday Adelaja
Embassy of God
Kiev, Ukraine

A letter to the General Reader

Hello dear Reader,

I am glad you have taken the interest to read this book but before you take the plunge, I will like to state here that the life stories of some people have been used to teach you some basic truths and principles and for the sake of their safety I have decided to use pen names instead of their real names. Let this be a contract between you and I that their personalities will be preserved and honoured. Also, you may probably need to ask yourself some questions and find sincere answers to them. This little exercise will help to prepare your mind in order to digest properly the expositions available in this book:

1) What drew your interest to read this book?
2) How will this interest be sustained?
3) What is your understanding of single ladies' stigmatization and how do you respond to it?
4) Will you be willing to learn from the contents (truths and principles) of this book?

Whatever your sincere answers are, I want to be your guide to discover how life should be for singles and the unmarried ladies. Come along!

A Letter to the Stigmatized Lady

Dear Friend,

First, I want to congratulate you because by the end of this book you will realize you are not what others have made you think you are. It will be helpful for you to take an inventory of who you are before reading this book and who you want to become after reading this book. After the thorough reading and exercises, you will begin to live the dignified life that you are ordained to live. Just promise yourself that you will gain every truth and principle in this book and work on your mind and whole self. Welcome to a whole new you!

**From the Author,
Esther Kuganja**

Table of Contents

Dedication ix
Acknowledgments xi
Foreword xiii
Introduction xix

Chapter 1: A Glimpse into the Life of A Single Lady 1
- The State of Being Single

Chapter 2: The Consequences and Foundation Laid by One's Childhood and Home Environment 11
- Lack of Role Models in a Home

Chapter 3: The Damage Caused by Culture and Societal Expectations 22
- Living the Imposed Vision

Chapter 4: The Damage Caused by Religiosity and Wrong Doctrines 35
- Most African Initiated Churches are Doing More Harm than Good

Chapter 5: Facing the Brutal Facts 51
- Why do We Have Many Single People in Our Societies Today?

Chapter 6: Examples of Great Achievers Despite Singleness 63
- Let Nothing Stop You from Becoming an Achiever

Chapter 7: The Journey of Self-discovery 76
- Discover the Treasure in You First,
  and then Others Will See it Too

Chapter 8: Learning to Let go and Finding Fulfilment While Single 89
- The Seemingly Hardest Decision,
  but the Most Liberating

Conclusion 99
The Power of Thriving and Shining
is in Your Mind and Hands; Use It!

End Notes 103
Bibliography 107
Other Services by the Author 109
About the Author 111
Contact details of the Author 112

Introduction

"*We wrestle with what we think we are not, rather than celebrate what we are.*"
Kate Coleman

Waking up to a quiet and bright Thursday morning, it was the 10th of November 2016, something was definitely different about this day. I felt joy unspeakable – it was my fortieth birthday! I was so full of gratitude to God and for life in general. I sat up in bed, reflecting on my life – I could see myself as a baby, young girl, a teenager, a university student and now a matured woman all in a space of four decades; it was incredible! I started counting my blessings: life, health, I could see several instances of divine intervention in my life, and so on.

Suddenly, it struck me that I never had these feelings a few years back. I was so blinded by my being single that I could not see anything positive about my life. In fact, I always avoided announcing or celebrating my birthdays, because I was afraid of people giving me that look: "*Oh… look at her, she is still single*", "*Could there be a reason why God is not answering her prayers?*" etc. I used to ask myself, "*Why celebrate if I don't seem to have achieved the society's expectations?*"

In this book, I share the processes that I went through, and the life-principles I have learnt from my mentor Dr. Sunday Adelaja, which I applied in order to overcome my struggles. I have previously been a member of a

Esther Kuganja

church where I experienced discrimination in leadership roles and tasks, just because of being single. How many women out there have great leadership potential, but are stereotyped and discriminated against? This book will address all these problems in our society today. It will open the eyes of leaders and the public in general, to the injustice that needs to be corrected, in order for the world to become a better and fairer place for all people, including those that are single.

"Most ladies suffer the stigma silently, because society seems to make them look odd or they later give in to pressure…. I yet believe God's word in Jeremiah 29:11 – 'For I know the thoughts that I think toward you, says the Lord, thoughts of peace and not of evil, to give you a future and a hope'. Everyone is on my neck over why I am not yet married. I have made up my mind to do it right or never. Some say I am choosy, which is not true; some say I don't socialize, which is not true - I grew up in a university environment, and was always involved in diverse young peoples' programmes. I have had relationships that didn't work, and none of the suitors has ever said I did anything to break up the relationship.

If you could see how all eyes get fixed on me anytime there is talk about late singleness, it can be scary - one would think I had an incurable disease. And the next thing you could ever imagine was to have someone come to put their hands on my head or hold my hand for prayers... I could go on and on telling my experiences. Many times I would weep much, not because I am not married, but because of the attitude of people towards me, especially those that I respect. I feel they should know better. These people side-line single folk even in the area of things they are capable of, as if marriage is a pre-requisite for ensuring that we make an impact and fulfil our destiny. But I know, "Though it may tarry, it will surely come to pass."

The above story is a real life experience of Susan*, a lady I met recently. I could not help thinking that thousands of us ladies are living with such pain. Is there no cause for a 'voice' to correct such stigmatisation, especially among Africans? It has become extremely difficult to live our lives free from people, and the 'system' around us constantly reminding us that something must be wrong with us to remain single late on in life. These negative stereotypes can be passed on either consciously or sub-consciously. As a result, many single women have wounds and hurts buried deeply, and only a book like this one can expose such. The only way to fight this injustice is by exposing it, talking about the problem and finding solutions, so that the next generation of women will not have to go through what some of us have gone through. This has made me even more determined to work on this book, in order to help ladies out there who are stigmatised, stereotyped and discriminated against because they are single.

"The pen is mightier than the sword."
– Edward Bulwer-Lytton

If you are a single lady (and most especially the older ones of thirty-five years and above):

This book will bring back your widest smile, brightest glow and self-esteem. It will enlighten you about the true meaning of life and its purpose. The book will take you through the stages of self-discovery, and re-alignment of your priorities. It will equip you with practical guidelines of how to live a fulfilled life despite the increased singleness in our world today. You will get to know people, who despite being single, have great achievements and legacies. You will discover that you are not alone.

To the relatives and friends of the single lady and the general public:

You will not only be shown the reality of the discrimination and the negative effect of the pressure put upon un-married women, but also be helped to adapt the right attitude to support them in fulfilling life's purpose.

To the Church leaders and all Christians:

You will discover the damage done by adopting wrong doctrines and attitudes towards single women. These doctrines are contrary to kingdom principles and we need to know how they can be corrected.

Believe me dear reader, that if I transitioned from being a desperate single to a now very happy and fulfilled woman, any single lady can too. This book is committed to taking any un-married woman from that state of anxiety and depression and pushing her into self-discovery and confidence. The truths contained within this book will help create a better world for single women. My desire is that this book will produce purposeful and kingdom-driven single ladies. Enjoy!

Esther Kuganja

Chapter 1

A Glimpse into the Life of A Single Lady

The State of Being Single

"Nobody can make you feel inferior without your consent."
Eleanor Roosevelt

In the introduction, I mentioned a quote from a friend named Susan. Her case is an example, amongst many others, that I intend to show you in this chapter, but first, let me take you into a journey of Genevieve*'s life.

After secondary school education, Genevieve was excited to start a new life at the university. It was September, and she had been admitted to study her first-choice course. At this time, she was a committed Christian and had strict moral values that were in place to preserve her whilst on campus. She wanted to be free from any parental influence, meet new friends, and carve out a career for herself. At age twenty-one, she was not thinking of marriage at all; her main focus was only on academic goals and ministerial outreaches.

The three years at the university went very fast. During the final year, she began to notice that most of her friends were already engaged or getting married. It suddenly dawned on her, that she must have been too

Esther Kuganja

serious to have neglected that part of her life. Yes, a few 'brothers' from the Christian fellowship of the university had approached her, but things just never worked out.

After graduating from the university, she was a supporter of her friends at their weddings, giving her best to make their special occasion a success. These weddings, which took place almost every weekend, were constant reminders of her single status. Panic set in as relatives started questioning her about this. It was obviously even more difficult to get suitors outside the university! *"Why can't people figure this out?"* Genevieve asked.

Three years after her graduation, she got an admission for postgraduate studies abroad. Even though it took her a while to get used to the new environment, she was very active in a Christian fellowship in the town, which helped her to settle down. A year later, she graduated and decided to stay in the country in the quest for opportunities, knowledge, and exposure. Genevieve observed in the church she attended, which was predominantly Nigerian, that the members were marrying only those from their own country, to the extent that some even went back to Africa to find a bride. Yet there were single ladies in the church! Then she wondered, *"Should I find a different church?"*

Well, in the town where Genevieve lived, there were very few people from her country of origin, compared to other cities. *"But I am helping and serving in the church here. I have friends here. This town is home to me. I cannot be hopping from train to train and church to church, in an attempt to search for a husband. Let the man find me wherever I am"* she thought. Nonetheless, she would visit different churches inside and outside the town she lived once in a while.

Again, there seemed to be no serious relationship working out for Genevieve, even when she decided to be open to any nationality, given her social environment. Each time she called her parents just to find out how they were doing, they would narrate to her the many weddings taking place. In other words, they intimated, *"When is your own?"* It reached a point when she stopped calling them for some time. She was just tired of the pressure and reminders of her single status. Her parents must have gotten the message – the wedding narratives ceased.

After thirteen years of living in the United Kingdom, Genevieve was still single. She was a victim of negative stereotyping, which affected her attitude towards life. This seemed to have prevented the right men from coming into her life. *"Could this be a curse?"* as some people would imagine. *"Maybe if she had gone back to her home country, she would be married by now." "Is God unfair? How can such a committed Christian not have her prayer answered by now?" "Is there something wrong with her?" "Is she destined to remain single?"*

Dear reader, I believe the answers to all these questions will be found in the following chapters of the book. Now imagine that you have come across an online platform, where single ladies share about their lives. Here are some examples of what you are likely to find. It is important that you take note of the different attitudes and the desperation of the characters, to help you appreciate the problem that this book is intended to address.

Justine*

I have spent forty-five years of my life without a husband. I was never married, not that I didn't want to be, but it just never happened. I always wanted to love and be loved since my youth, but I didn't feel so loved by the boyfriends I had, at least to the point of getting married to any of them.

Now, though I am forty-five, I still feel like I am twenty. I have come to the understanding that I must love myself first before I can share that love with someone else. I have gone through various kinds of therapies to get me going and to accept myself, but you know, it is very hard and I feel I am losing myself. I really want a good man. I don't think I can continue this way for the next five years. It is so intimidating to continue to be single.

Phoebe*

Hello there! I can't imagine why so many of us singles are lamenting over our status. I am single and loving it! Standing before the mirror, I feel more beautiful and sexier than I was at either my early youth or five years ago. And guess what. I just clocked forty.

At my age, I am a free bird. I go wherever I want and whenever I want, without having to be monitored or feel guilty by any man. Last year I spent two months on Cuban beaches and touring Rome; my life is just in my hands. I don't have to pretend in the presence of anyone about my looks or how I dress. I am just who I am. Why should I be bothered about marrying a man, who pretends to love me head-over-heels, yet is looking at other women's figures? It is reality, and I am not sounding off.

Terry*

I usually don't do this, but I am happy to see single ladies express themselves on this platform. I am an Indian woman in my early forties. It is so surprising how time has flown by. I never found a man to whom we would tie the knot, and looking through my early days, all I could see were Indian parents wanting to get me a husband. (You must understand the Indian culture of arranged marriage.) But I never wanted any of it. They just didn't please me.

Funny enough, I am still very young at heart and still want that tingly feeling of love from a true heart. Now that I am independent, I have my work as my passion and my parents to look after, as they are really old. I feel very lonely, and even friends don't help because they are all married. When we get together, all they get to speak about are the ups and downs of their love affairs or their children, forgetting that my ears are full of them. I hope they will realize my pains and pity me.

And here is a word to the men who are here on this platform: I am not writing this to attract any of you. It is just a means to pour out my distress. I am even surprised I could go this far to spew all this out. So shoo!

My Letter to Dr Sunday Adelaja
29 October 2016

Dear Ps. Sunday:

I just want to say a *big thank-you* personally for the teachings on women. Today, when you were about to mention 'why some women were still single,' I was all ears waiting for an answer I had never heard before. And there it came. "It is because you have not found a man who has recognized and appreciated your uniqueness." Tears were running down my face, and I exclaimed, "At last I am delivered!"

Next month I will be turning forty. I am still single and a virgin. I became a Christian at age twelve, and all my life the reasons for my singleness that I have been hearing from people who have been around me have been the following:

- You are cursed or under an evil covenant.
- You don't wear make-up.
- You don't wear tight-fitting clothes.
- You need to go to the gym (meaning you are too fat).
- You are too educated.
- You don't smile all the time.
- You are not social.

Well, I came to believe all these reasons all my life until 2013, when I started listening to your audio teachings.

No one has ever told me the only true reason until today! I wept because of the hurt buried within me that I did not even know was still there, even though I have embraced my singleness as a gift from God and am now focusing on my purpose (thanks to your teachings).

Thank you, Pastor, for bringing healing to my whole being. I love myself more, I am more joyful and confident these days than ever before because at last someone has told me the truth - YOU!

Esther Kuganja
Leamington Spa

Dear reader, it is very interesting to contrast the attitudes of Justine and Phoebe. We also find in the letter, that a lot of negativity surrounding a single lady can influence her mindset. I hope that these examples have given you a glimpse into the life of a single lady. You can now put yourself in the characters' situations and wonder what you would have done differently.

This chapter has shed some light on the negativity that

can surround any single lady if care is not taken. In the next chapter, let me take you on a journey to discover how important the roles of parents are in modelling an ideal home and marriage to a child, and how this can affect attitudes to marriage.

Character Aroma Nuggets Part 1:

1) Understand that some ladies are single because of circumstances beyond their control, for example moving abroad to a new environment, career advancement or ill health.
2) Single ladies need to adapt a positive attitude towards life in general. This helps to attract the good and right things in their lives.
3) It is advisable to create or move to a positive environment that boosts one's faith and flushes negativity from the mind. What type of messages or friends are you listening to? Are they pushing you towards your life-purpose?
4) *"Single moms: You are a doctor, a teacher, a nurse, a maid, a cook, a referee, a heroine, a provider, a defender, a protector, a true Superwoman. Wear your cape proudly."* — Mandy Hale
5) Young people, work on yourself, and then consider the person you want to attract in terms of character, love, integrity, intellectual abilities, etc.
6) Your virginity is a precious gift from God and should not be thrown to 'pigs' but be preserved for the ordained 'Prince'. If there is no man who qualifies and has worked on themselves to acquire the 'Prince' title, then keep your gift to yourself and get busy in moving your life forward. We are in a world where some people are busy improving their lives through self-education, mentorship, character development, and so on, whilst others are laid back, praying for a partner without preparing themselves to be the best spouse. The latter group does not deserve the blessing of a successful relationship because of the violation of this principle of life: sowing and reaping.
7) *"Do not give dogs what is sacred; do not throw your pearls to pigs. If you do, they may trample*

them under their feet, and turn and tear you to pieces" - Matthew 7:6 (NKJV)
8) *"Happily single is holding out for the best and letting go of the rest. It's saying "I will and I can" to yourself before you say "I do" to someone else."* ― Mandy Hale
9) *"I want to be known as the 23 year-old who is foolishly in love with a Prince she can't see. I want to rejoice while holding the rose of singleness, even when my hands bleed from its thorns. I want to resist the urge to envy the pairs growing in the middle of my neighbours' gardens. I want to be rooted in the simple truth that unripe pairs taste like lies and lingering loneliness. I want to put Jesus on my bullet-wound and cling to His heart wrenching hope because He was kind enough to be a Band-Aid when He should have stayed a King."* ― Katie Kiesler
10) Let us not rush to judge the single ladies around us; they already have enough trouble in their lives without our contribution. Showing love and support can go a long way to heal their wounds and insecurities.

Recall and Deliberate (Part 1)

<u>To the general reader</u>

Take a break and think for a while:

- a) How have you been envisioning or treating late single ladies?
- b) Do you think it is right for them to be stigmatized?
- c) If you were still single, how would you feel and what would you do differently?
- d) What are the ways you think you can change the perception that others around you in your family, community or church have about late singles or the unmarried?
- e) How will this change affect the late singles or what ways will it change the pressure of getting married at all cost?

<u>To the Stigmatized Single Lady</u>

Stand in front of a mirror, gaze into it - what do you see? If who you see is the same as who you used to think you were before you read this chapter, then you may need to put this book down, take a walk and ponder on what you have read. But if the few pages have pricked your heart then it means you have begun this exciting journey.

Chapter 2

The Consequences and Foundation Laid by One's Childhood and Home Environment

Lack of Role Models in a Home

> *"I am even crying here because this is not fiction, and many people are frightened away from marriage because of observed or experienced abuse."*
> Precious Jemibewon

In the previous chapter, we looked at the life of a single lady, but we shouldn't forget that any lady was once a child, in the custody of parents or guardians. It is generally said that we are a product of our environment. How true! In this chapter, we are going to look at the negative effects of one's childhood environment and address the lack of role models in the lives of children and young people. We shall see traces of this in Genevieve's background below – highlighting factors that contribute to negative foundations in a child's life that cause problems in later life.

a) Single-sex Schools

Throughout her primary and secondary education, Genevieve attended only girls' boarding schools. In those days, it was thought that such a strategy caused girls to concentrate on their studies as they were 'protected' from the boys. As a matter of fact, the best schools were actually single-sex schools. So it was understandable that Genevieve's parents wanted the best for her. As good as the intentions of her parents were, such protection could hinder a child's development in relationships; girls may end up not being themselves around the opposite sex and find it difficult to engage in the real world. This applies to the boys-only school too. Students are not exposed to a rich social life and therefore find it difficult to approach ladies.

In her article: *16 tell-tale signs you went to an all-girls school*, Victoria Lambert, an American award-winning journalist, said: *"You date your boss. Where else do you meet men?" "You date your cleaner. Where else do you meet men?"* So you find that many ladies who went to a same-sex school struggle to get a right partner and worse still, can end up falling into the wrong hands. As a young girl, Genevieve lacked confidence around men and often escaped to church activities, the library or solitude. Most of the time, her social life was limited.

b) Absenteeism of Parents

Genevieve does not recall much of her mother being constantly available whilst she was growing up, most especially before the age of six. Her parents obviously had marital problems that frequently drove her mother away from the home. Her dad would go to work each day and come back in the evening, so she grew up mainly around house maids plus some relatives, and missed the loving environment of both parents. Genevieve became a very reserved girl, never talked much, obviously a lack of self-esteem had popped into her personality. At some point in time, her mother came back home and life was much better (please note that the damage had already been done at a very sensitive stage of her development).

The fact that all Genevieve's siblings went to boarding schools most of the time, explains why there was no real closeness in the family. It seemed like everyone lived their own lives, and were closer to their own friends. Although the family never lacked the basic necessities of clothing, food, shelter and school fees (a credit to her hardworking father); there was an absence of parents, a lack of intentional family quality time and a death of bonding exercises in the family.

Let me pause here, to point out that we all possess the general fallen human nature so there shouldn't be any blame game. Some of our parents were raised in homes where good values and principles were neither passed on nor modelled. Even if there was an attempt to teach life-governing values such as never to steal, tell lies, commit adultery, kill and so on, these were passed on as head-knowledge as opposed to real understanding.

c) Marital Unfaithfulness and its Implications

During Genevieve's childhood, she grew fonder of her father and saw him as her hero in many ways. She always looked forward to his return from work, to feel that sense of fatherly security in the home, and sometimes there were surprises – that always put a smile on her face! At about the age of seven, Genevieve was introduced to other girls, and was told they were her sisters (not many details were given). On the one hand, she was glad to have company as her elder brother was always away in boarding school, but on the other hand, she was confused – how could she have sisters? Who are their father and mother? Later on, as she grew more in understanding, she began to distrust her father and men in general. *"They can't be trusted!"* she thought.

Infidelity in the home can have multiple repercussions – Genevieve's mother was emotionally wounded and often released her frustrations through being tough and hard on Genevieve - the eldest daughter. Resentment grew even more in Genevieve's heart. Who could she talk to? No one! She rarely smiled. – This became a habit even into adulthood. No one ever asked; "why?" The much needed psychological help was never offered. She developed negative emotions of rejection, anger, bitterness, poor self-image and low self-esteem. See how just one mistake can impact a child so drastically!

> *"A person is, among all else, a material thing, easily torn and not easily mended."*
> - Ian McEwan, Atonement

d) Parental Pressure

In her book: '*7 Deadly Sins of Women in Leadership*', Kate Coleman mentions how her mother asked someone to help search for a suitable man to complete Kate's life (pg. 129). This is a common practice for most parents, especially in Africa and Asia, where children are of age and yet they hear no marriage plans from them – to such parents, marriage is a societal status that must be attained by everybody!

Taking you back to Genevieve's story, I did mention that she used to call her parents to check on them frequently. Oftentimes, the response would be something like, "*We are fine. Your cousin is getting married this weekend. We attended our friend's daughter's traditional introduction ceremony last weekend and a lot of weddings are coming up in the next months …*" and so on and so forth. Well, if care is not taken parents could push their children into making wrong decisions that could cause a lot of heartache, all because of parental pride. Parents want to show off to their mates that their children are getting married. My advice to all parents is to be supportive through prayers and friendship. If any parent has not *intentionally* raised their child to be successful in marriage and modelled an ideal married life to them, then they have no business pushing them into marriage in the first place.

Here are some advices to the single ladies (and gentlemen) whose parents are bothering them with the marriage question:

- Let your parents know your thoughts about the matter – after all it's your life and you know what you want at that point in your life more than they do.
- Help them understand that you have personal life-governing principles and are happy to do things your way.
- It is good to ask your parents some questions and to hear them out. This boosts mutual understanding and eases any concerns.

e) The Lack of Role Models

Genevieve was naturally an observant child. She confided that her mother would sometimes play the happy wife in public but in the real fact she was obviously hurting. When it came to Genevieve's extended family, oh my... it was chaos. *"Is marriage really worth it?"* she would ask. Here are some examples:

- A member of the extended family passed away and left many children that he had with different women. Others were never known. It looked like he had a 'wife' in every district! It was a shock when they turned up for the burial ceremony. This man did not leave even a 'penny' as inheritance for his children. Instead, some men praised him as a hero for having children. The question is, *"Was he competing with pigs and cats? Because they too can win this competition!"* In his will, he just stated, "I have left my children to the clan." Such cases of high degree of irresponsibility

are very common in Africa. "*Are there no more responsible men?*" "*Do men just use women to satisfy their sexual desires and then leave them – just like that?*" "*How come nobody is speaking out against such behaviour?*"
- Looking at Genevieve's entire extended family, there were many cases of unfaithfulness in marriage with very few exceptions. She could count on one hand the marriages that were 'good'. Some men would end up impregnating house maids, relatives of the wife who would come to live with them or just have affairs outside the home, etc. There were many such stories.
- At about the age of twelve, Genevieve witnessed a neighbour attacking another woman by pouring water at her, chasing her out of the house. The two were fighting over a man, who was less concerned and stayed inside the house whilst the two women's noise disturbed the whole neighbourhood. "*Is that man really worth this fight?*" "*Why isn't he coming out to stop the nonsense?*" Genevieve thought.
- When it came to newspapers that Genevieve read, oh my… every day had several stories of domestic abuse, acid attacks and murder – all related to jealousy, control of women by their husbands, and so on.

When a child is exposed to all these 'dramas' how do we expect them to view marriage positively? How will they look forward to marriage without some fears and doubts? Role models are a necessity in the lives of all our children so that they can have a positive outlook and be the best spouses in the future.

In this chapter, we have looked at some factors experienced during childhood and in the home environment. These can cause damage to the psyche of any person, especially in their approach to marriage.

I call upon all parents and guardians to pay extra care to the environment of your children. In the next chapter, we shall look at how culture and societal expectations play a role in the life of a single lady. Keep reading!

Character Aroma Nuggets Part 2:

1) Think before you act because others are watching, and decisions have far greater effects than you could ever imagine.
2) Throughout the stages of a child's development, it is important for parents to surround them with an environment of love, peace and acceptance.
3) When parents are so busy working that they have no time for their children, they will end up being raised by strangers – house maids or care givers, whose background may be unknown. And then the parents will never bond with their children.
4) Parents, if you want to raise godly children, who will have a strong foundation to face the future, then you need to *intentionally* create time (say thirty minutes to an hour) every day, to instill the right values in them.
5) Fathers are the first male figures in the lives of the girls. They have the responsibility to model a true gentleman to their daughters. So unconditional love and common courtesies to a lady must be demonstrated. Then in the future, the daughter would easily identify the right man for her.
6) *"When it comes to your personal life, take advice, don't take orders"* - Dr. Bien Sufficient
7) When you find yourself in a dysfunctional family, stop and say to yourself, *"Even though my parents have failed to be good parents, I will do things differently and be a better parent to my own children"*. When this decision is made, then run with it and prove it not only to yourself but to God who has entrusted you with your own family.
8) Parents - take time to study your children and identify their needs. We should not take our family members for granted and assume that all is well!
9) In most African cultures, parents never apologise to their children. So when offended, these children

tend to bottle-up a lot of anger and resentment. These issues need to be addressed. It is a simple courtesy to apologise to anyone we offend, even if they are our own children. The fact remains that they are human beings with feelings just like us.

10) When acting out of character, stop and take time out to ask: Why am I reacting like this? Could it be because of my problem with my spouse? Parents, it is important to be consciously aware of yourself, and not to pour out all your frustrations onto your children. This is most common with mothers, who have been hurt by their husbands. Please seek professional help to heal emotionally or to manage your anger. The days of ignorance are now over. There is information for anyone who seeks it.

Esther Kuganja

Recall and Deliberate (Part 2)

<u>To the general reader</u>

a) Are you a parent with your child in a single sex school? How much of the detailed knowledge do you have about the school that you have made your child to be attending?
b) Would you consider also the downsides of having to study in a single sex school and its short and long term effect on you children?
c) Are you a single parent or a divorcee? Have you taken into account the negative toll it will have on the upbringing of your children?
d) Do you think to wait on time and chance, your extended family, guardian or the society to guide and care for your children is a wise idea?
e) To the one cheating on your spouse, have you taken into consideration what negative messages you are also sending to your children?
f) Parents who want their sons and daughters married at all cost, do you recognize that they are full human beings, capable of making their own decisions? Have you taken time to understand your children and their preferences? Do you recognize what trouble they are trying to avoid?
g) Take time to assess your decisions (both in the past and the nearest future). What image are these decisions building in the minds of your children, spouse, family and the society at large? You may really need to rethink your decisions, actions or inactions.

<u>To the Stigmatized Single Lady</u>

Take an account of how any of the issues discussed in this chapter (and those that you personally went through) have marred your image and self-esteem. To what extent is this psychological, emotional and social distortion?

Take a decision to forgive anyone who has hurt you before and move on. For healing to come to you, you must recognize what the cause of your trouble is, and decide to let go of the stress it has procured. Only do not allow this same kind of environment to pull you down anymore.

Chapter 3

The Damage Caused by Culture and Societal Expectations

Living the Imposed Vision

"Imposed vision is what women live out when they focus on trying to be something that someone else wants them to be. Many women feel guilty if they fail to fulfil the demands of others or else they may fear being thought of as selfish or self-indulgent."
Kate Coleman

In this chapter, we are going to examine the negative effects of culture and societal expectations on the lives of women and later conclude that we all need to get into marriage because of our understanding and not because of traditions. I have included some statistics to give you a clear picture of what is going on around the world concerning women, sex, and marriage.

The United Nations Children's Fund (UNICEF) estimates that two-fifth of all African girls are married before the age of eighteen. In some countries, the proportion is much higher. For example, in Chad and Niger, a third of young women aged twenty to twenty-four said they were married by the age of fifteen[1]. In most rural African communities, Government efforts are seen in trying to educate children through the Universal Primary and Secondary Education, which is free. But in reality, most girls are likely to drop-out due to a number of reasons:

- The cultural pressure to get married while young is still widespread. An example is the story of Bintasy, a Senegalese lady, who was forced into marriage at just thirteen years and had her first child at sixteen. Today, she is campaigning to prevent forced marriages[2].
- The high level of irresponsibility amongst parents, who think that girls should not be a financial burden on the family, because they will hopefully belong to another man in the nearby future!
- Most families are under pressure to give birth to boys since they are seen as future breadwinners. Funds are invested in them rather than in the girls.
- If parents are not well or eventually die, daughters are expected to stay at home and do the domestic work, look after the sick, plant some crops in the garden for the family and so on. These responsibilities make it difficult for the girls to concentrate on studies.

"The parents, family and society put so much pressure on young people to get married. Marriage today to some people has become like an achievement!"
– Dr. Bien Sufficient

"Custom in Africa is stronger than domination, stronger than the law, stronger even than religion. Over the years, customary practices have been incorporated into religion, and ultimately have come to be believed by their practitioners to be demanded by their adopted gods, whoever they may be"
- Lightfoot-Klein

For most people, the stages of life can be illustrated as follows:

| 1 Birth | 2 Education | 3 Career | 4 Marriage | 5 Death |

Some years back (and even today in some cases), some rural communities especially in the developing world did not emphasise stages two and three above for girls. There was a popular belief that having daughters was a source of wealth achieved through 'bride-price.' What a tragedy! We need to fight this mind-set and stamp it out of our communities for good. The belief that girls are born to prepare to become wives and mothers exists in almost all societies of the world. The difference we see now in the twenty-first century is that some societies chose to outgrow their old and undesirable ways, while other societies have chosen to remain stuck. We should not elevate culture above the needed wisdom and understanding of our times.

Here is another evidence of societal expectations - while on a visit to Germany in October 2016, the Nigerian President Muhammadu Buhari made an astonishing statement: *"I don't know which party my wife belongs to, but she belongs to my kitchen and my living room and the other room"*[3]. If this can come from a member of the elite group in the twenty-first century, I worry! Traditions and cultures were started by man and can be undone by man. It starts with an individual and then the family, and once a family is a good example, other people in the community will emulate them. The community begins to change and eventually the whole nation.

Let's examine some world statistics:

Table 1: The Average Age People Lose their Virginity around the World (44 countries) by Alfie Powell, October, 2016[4]

Rank	Country	Average Age	Rank	Country	Average Age
1	Iceland	15.6	23	Netherlands	18.1
2	Denmark	16.1	24	Canada	18.1
3	Sweden	16.2	25	Switzerland	18.2
4	Norway	16.5	26	United Kingdom	18.3
5	Finland	16.5	27	France	18.5
6	Israel	16.7	28	South Africa	18.7
7	Bulgaria	16.9	29	Mexico	18.7
8	Portugal	16.9	30	Russia	18.7
9	Belgium	17.2	31	Taiwan	18.9
10	Chile	17.2	32	Italy	18.9
11	Czech Republic	17.2	33	Poland	19.0
12	Austria	17.3	34	Indonesia	19.1
13	Croatia	17.3	35	Spain	19.2
14	Ireland	17.3	36	Japan	19.4
15	Brazil	17.4	37	Nigeria	19.7
16	Germany	17.6	38	Vietnam	19.7
17	Slovakia	17.8	39	Hong Kong	20.2
18	New Zealand	17.8	40	Thailand	20.5
19	Turkey	17.8	41	China	22.1
20	Australia	17.9	42	Singapore	22.8
21	United States	18.0	43	India	22.9
22	Greece	18.1	44	Malaysia	23.0

Table 1 above shows us that sexual activity starts as early as fifteen years of age (and even less). So the general impression is that anyone who is not married or has no partner by thirty looks out of place. After the age of twenty, a person is seen as abnormal not to have had any sexual encounter at all. Such individuals are seen as weird, old fashioned and inexperienced. This can stigmatize many people, forcing them to give in at any given opportunity.

Table 2: Countries with the lowest mother's mean age at first birth[5]

Rank	Country	Average Age
1	Angola	18.0
2	Bangladesh, Niger	18.1
3	Chad	18.2
4	Mali	18.6
5	Guinea, Uganda, Mozambique, Malawi	18.9
6	Liberia, Gaza Strip, Botswana, Sierra Leone	19.0
7	Zambia	19.2
8	Sao Tome, Principe, Burkina Faso	19.4
9	Cabo Verde, Madagascar, Swaziland	19.5
10	Tanzania, Ethiopia	19.6

From the table above, we can deduce that many young ladies get into relationships and become mothers without planning for the child or being mentally, emotionally and financially ready for the baby. Culture and societal expectations have pushed many young people into situations they were not prepared for.

I hope by now, dear reader, that you have an idea of general cultures and societal expectations concerning women, sex and marriage. I recently read an article: *If You Want a Rich Husband, Be a Rich Wife*[6] by Dr. Bien Sufficient. In this article, the riches she referred to were not in monetary terms but richness in values such as love, purpose and vision, discipline and character. She advised that for anyone to become someone in life, they ought to say 'no' to societal pressures.

As logical people, we need to understand where we are coming from in order for us to know where we ought to be or to be going. Most of our traditions and customs were started by our forefathers, many generations past, who did not know God, the Author of Life and the purpose of life itself. We are supposed to be followers of the Author of Life and not followers of people and their man-made cultures. Please do not get me wrong here - some of the practices in different cultures are really good; for example, showing respect and honour to parents or elders, but other beliefs that are counterproductive and primitive in nature, ought to be discarded.

> ***"We have been engineered culturally to believe we are nothing without fruitfulness of the womb. You might as well be dead. What a myth!"***
> - Fünmie Jébōdà

I get stunned at the boldness of some people. They can just come up to you and ask, *"Why are you still single?"* Secretly I would like to shout back, *"Mind your own business!"* But over the years, I have come to understand where they are coming from and to take my time to answer their question. And there could be different answers depending on the person asking. I have been part of singles groups and even lead one. I have interacted with many single people of both sexes and you would be amazed at how they answer this question. Here is a selection of responses:

- *"Well, I don't really know!"*
- *"I have not met the right person yet"*
- *"I am still concentrating on my studies and career"*
- *"Marriage is not for me"*
- *"I am too busy really, I have no social life"*
- *"You just don't understand; I cannot approach a woman, it freaks me out!"*
- *"Maybe am not so beautiful and attractive enough"*
- *"It could be that I am invisible - no man notices me!"*

- "There are no men around - in my church everyone is married!"
- "It must be a curse; they say I need prayers"

"I'm single because I was born that way."
- Mae West

I would like to mention here that I like Mae's response. She's got a point – we are all born single. Yes, our destinies and callings are specific to us as individuals, and the sooner we understand this, the better. Therefore, when one gets married, they also have to remain single, that is; maintain and not lose their personality and individuality.

While listening to Dr. Sunday Adelaja's teaching entitled: *'Why all Brides dress like a Princess'*, he gave the only true reason why any woman that is single is so, and this is the only reason I adopted as my own: *"You have not found a man who has recognised and appreciated your uniqueness!"* This was it for me – all the other 'nonsense' reasons that negativity and the environment had labelled me with had to be dropped there and then. It was a great deliverance for me. I wept tears because of the pain that was unknowingly buried within me but I also wept tears of joy. A peacefulness just swept over me; I knew my life had changed forever – there was no more looking back.

Now, let's reflect on why we often feel victims of this societal pressure. I took some clues from a beloved writer Kim Quindlen in her article: *'17 Reasons We Constantly Feel Pressured to Get Engaged before we're Ready'*[7]. Here goes:

Societal Standards over Fading Youthfulness

Most cultures preach to youngsters that they should get married earlier because time is not usually on the side of ladies, as their youthfulness fades quickly and men don't usually find them attractive afterwards. This is a short-sighted way of viewing life. Youths should be proud of the knowledge and wisdom accumulated over the years and their resourcefulness, as this is a beauty that never fades.

Misconception about Marriage

To many, marriage is just an event - an occasion that should or must be fulfilled. So once it is done it is checked out of their to-do list. How sad! This is why most marriages fail. People organize big parties and make a noise and get praises instead of getting praised for doing the right things or marrying the right person for the right purpose. People should never be directly or indirectly taught this myth.

Generally Expected Cycle

Each community has a fixed pattern to which people must live and what they must achieve at certain points of their lives. Milestones like getting an admission to a higher institution, graduation, finding a job and of course getting married. There is almost no place for discovering potentials or pursuing dreams, instead concentration is demanded in getting high remuneration, or excellent grades and such pursuits are usually temporal.

The Deception Involved in Weddings

As seen on media and all around us, we are carried away by the end products of preparation for a one day's wedding alone, meanwhile almost no attention is paid to whether we are ready for the marriage in question or its demands.

Being Overburdened by Tempting Questions

Are you in a relationship? Aren't you going to get married?

When will you ring the marriage bells? These are questions you might have been burdened with at several points in your life and they point to nothing other than for you to escape or quit the life of singleness even if people do not say it plainly - but at least that is what they imply. The sad thing is they make the youths feel as if there is no value in being single or that there is so much more that marriage has to offer compared to being single. This is absurd! And come to think of it, the same set of people will never be there when your marriage hits the rocks.

The Deceitfulness of Marriage Displays

By watching celebrations alone of marriages conducted in several places or by standing in front of a seamstress shop staring at a beautiful wedding gown, can make many daydream and plan for or book some items needed for a wedding, to which there is no right candidate yet. Right from childhood, weddings have been so ingrained in people's minds as some form of activity or event that is the most important day of our lives.

The Unavoidability of Love Stories

Even though we determine not to dance to the tunes of people's expectations of us, we cannot stop them from coming to us, even indirectly through advertisements and displays on the media. For those who watch movies or television, they become an easy target – their emotions get involved with the idea of getting engaged or getting married, or at least cheering a friend who is already married.

Lack of Understanding of the Purpose of a Single Lady's Life

It is sad to have others discourage singles, especially ladies, from pursuing their passions, by making them think they are just past times. And those milestones like getting married or rearing children are the main duty of a woman. This is totally a lack of understanding of what the single lady is capable of using her years for.

Information Age

In this jet age, society can easily monitor people and the person trying to keep on with his or her single life can easily be pressurised especially through mobile phones and social media. Two decades ago, this was not so except for a few prompters given occasionally to singles here and there at socials or functions. This present opportunity can be pushy to the singles.

Reconnecting with Old Buddies

Family members, relatives or old friends, who we reconnect with after a long time due to advancement in study or work, try to catch up with us and the few matters that come up in their minds is usually about work and love lives. One can't blame them though, but they should also know that there are other areas that could be of interest to single people, and that is worth more talking about.

Insensitivity of Well-wishers

Have you ever been at that point where you are just tired of other people, especially the old folks, pointing a finger at you after a wedding ceremony with the words, 'you are next', even though it is for good? Well that alone is enough pressure to get married to just any one who comes your way.

Unnecessary Pitying Faces

In a similar way, it can be unappealing to see pitying faces staring at you, because of your long endured status, not having an understanding that in actual sense there is a beauty in the wait. No matter how concerned people may be, they need to understand that it doesn't help matters at all, rather it makes things worse.

This has been quite an in-depth chapter, with the intention of expressing the facts and reality of our world today. I hope, dear reader, that by now you appreciate the kind of pressure unmarried women can face on a daily basis. In the next chapter, we are going to further look at the damage caused by churches (mostly African Initiated Churches) through religiosity and wrong doctrines. If you are not a Christian, please do not skip the next chapter, it is such an enlightenment. On the other hand, if you are a Christian or Church leader, then the next chapter may interest you more!

Character Aroma Nuggets Part 3:

1) *"Don't allow the approval of others to obstruct your view of yourself."* – Bob Gass
2) Forget what people are thinking about you. You can't change that, so focus on what you can change – you and your thoughts.
3) Young ladies, please seek wisdom, understanding and 'maturity' before your moment of decision and choice to get married.
4) *"Seek to be you, the rest won't matter. Do not let the environment make you into a lie, do not let people's expectations make you into who you are not."* – Success Olayemi Fakolade
5) *"Know who you are or someone else will tell you!"* – Anon
6) *"There are no short-cuts to maturity"* – Rick Warren
7) *"Your attitude, not your achievements, brings happiness."* – Bob Gass
8) *"If you don't understand the purpose of a thing (e.g. marriage), then abuse is inevitable."* – Dr. Myles Munroe
9) The basic human needs are:

    a) Acceptance (that you are needed)
    b) Identity (that you are special)
    c) Security (protection, care)
    d) Purpose (for your life) - Dr. Creflo Dollar

10) *"A confident attitude and strong willpower is what you need to not succumb to marriage pressure*[8]*"* - Rituparna Roy Deshpande

Esther Kuganja

Recall and Deliberate (Part 3)

<u>To the general reader</u>

a) What is your perception of the feminine gender?
b) What are the cultural values that you or others around you have or uphold towards girls and women locally and internationally? Are these values helping or demeaning them?
c) What are your thoughts on early marriages and their impact on girls and women?
d) Shouldn't women be allowed to live their lives and given the chance to decide to get married when they are of full maturity - psychologically, emotionally and socially?
e) What are the ways you think this societal ill can be corrected?
f) How can you personally create an awareness to educate and bring change to your own community or environment?

<u>To the Stigmatized Single Lady</u>

It is sad that you are where you are because of the society you find yourself in. But you must recognize that you are an individual that is responsible for yourself. What happens to you is usually as a result of what you permit yourself. This is why you must take an inventory of who you are before you began reading this book and who you want to become after reading this book. Be truthful to yourself because it is all about you now, not about the society any more.

Chapter 4

The Damage Caused by Religiosity and Wrong Doctrines

Most African Initiated Churches are Doing More Harm than Good

> *Knowing the correct password - saying 'Master, Master,' for instance - isn't going to get you anywhere with me. What is required is serious obedience - doing what my Father wills. I can see it now - at the Final Judgment thousands strutting up to me and saying, 'Master, we preached the Message, we bashed the demons, our God-sponsored projects had everyone talking.' And do you know what I am going to say? 'You missed the boat. All you did was use me to make yourselves important. You don't impress me one bit. You're out of here.*
> Matthew 7:22-23 MSG

In this chapter, with specific emphasis on Pentecostal or Charismatic African Initiated Churches (AICs) - which are started and controlled by Africans,[9] we shall look at how wrong doctrines and attitudes towards single ladies have caused more harm than good. This is really sad because the church is supposed to be a solution-provider to communities and not the source of any problem.

My concerns with African Initiated Churches (AICs):

1. Demonology Doctrines

Having been a Christian for about twenty-eight years now, I have been exposed to all sorts of teachings and doctrines. There comes a time in life when one takes a step back to examine one's life and what one believes. I have studied the Bible (a Christian standard guide) for myself and as a thinking person; I have come to understand a few things. While I believe that demons exist, (in fact when I come across a demonic situation, I address it there and then as an inspired Christian and then move on with my business). I do not build a 'nest' over demons or the demonic situation day in and day out. I am too busy for that. Life must move on. My concern therefore is about people 'majoring' in the 'minors' and 'minoring' in the 'majors'. When we leave out the most important things in life and start focusing on the wrong things, we are derailed. As a single lady, if you believe that the cause of your singleness is demons, and you go for every prayer meeting in town for years, and nothing has changed, it's time to question what you have believed.

> "So many people are dying in ignorance. I know one lady who was placed on a six months deliverance scheme for a pattern of late marriage that runs in her family. Her pastor initiated this programme, yet this woman is still not yet married after undergoing the deliverance. Only this truth will set her free."
> - Nekky Okoro

As messages on life-purpose are getting fewer these days, the ones on breakthrough (in terms of marriage, immigration status and finances) are at their highest, because the church is actually encouraging and producing miracle-minded members. The same applies to the testimonies and prayer requests given in churches today, especially African churches. I will give a few real life examples here:

- *"Hallelujah! Brethren, God has done it again… I now have a visa!"*
- *"Praise… praise… praise the Lord!"* Showing off her ring, this lady continues, *"I am now engaged and the wedding is only three months away! I prophesy to all the singles here today, your turn is coming soon, hallelujah?"* And the whole congregation shouts a very loud: *"Amen!"*
- *"God is good all the time! I thank God for my breakthrough – I now have a 9-5 job! Glory be to God!"*
- *"Let us pray for our single sisters here, that their husbands will locate them by fire…prayer!"*
- *"Every curse in their lives, that is not allowing them to be noticed by men, be broken in Jesus name!"*
- *"Every evil veil that is covering your head, catch fire!"*
- *"Every spirit husband troubling this sister, claiming her as a wife – die… die… die… die by fire!"*

"Our youth must know that Christianity is not magic. We must tell them that because somebody is making pronunciations doesn't mean that those pronunciations are godly. We must let them know that they don't need a pastor's blessing to make it in life. We must let our young people know that the shout of "I receive it!" alone is not enough to be blessed for that week. We must open their eyes to realize that the shout of "Amen" no matter how loud, doesn't make God fulfil all their wishes. Our nation needs to be delivered

> ***from religious superstitions, and real Christianity must be introduced afresh."***[10]
> – Dr. Sunday Adelaja

Now tell me dear reader, with this kind of environment, what more can you expect but to see single ladies panicking in fear and void of purpose. I remember a certain incident that happened to me some years back. My housemates (at the time) and I heard about a deliverance service featuring a man of God from Nigeria taking place at a local church. The advert convinced us that all our problems could be sorted out at the meeting. Two of us were singles while the other mate had issues with her immigration status. We were warned that in that church, no one comes in wearing trousers, and with their head not covered (for women only - I wondered why women always had to be oppressed with such laws). Well, we obeyed the instructions, but in my mind I thought, *"Hmm… So is God only in the building and not out there on the streets? Are my prayers only answered while in this church and covered up, but not when I am elsewhere?"*

Off we went for the breakthrough church service. There was singing of praise and worship which was fine by me, then came the fiery prayers of binding and losing. I almost lost my voice as we were told to shout as loudly as we possibly could. Phew!! I can still recall the stress. *"Why did Jesus die for me if I have to sweat like this with these 'demons'?"* I thought. Then came my turn for the one-to-one session. The minister poured oil on my head and as he prayed, I tried very hard to ignore the spit coming from his mouth while he shouted into my face. He told me to drink some oil, poured some in my ears. He then hit my back hard with his hands, as he called out the demons and spun me round until I became dizzy and fell to the floor. It is so painful remembering all this. Believe me friend, when I finally walked out of that church, I vowed never to enter another one or associate myself with such a denomination – enough was enough!

How a Single Woman Can Overcome Stigmatisation

I have come to believe that not every challenge or setback is demonic. When you have prayed all forms of prayer, fasting and personal retreats, and still nothing changes, then be still and relax. Stop fighting God! The teachings about witchcraft and curses being responsible for older women remaining single births more fear in people and hatred for family members than any other subject. Is this doctrine promoting the love of God? This should indicate whether the leaders of such congregations are really of God! Having gained more insight into God's word and his will for my life, I have become more conscious and selective about who I follow or listen to.

> **"If I were to remain silent, I'd
> be guilty of complicity."**
> - Albert Einstein

I have witnessed AIC's where there is a much greater emphasis and focus on what the devil is doing in people's lives than on what God is doing. It is sad. People are then misled into believing that their 'sorrow and suffering' is due to witchcraft done by their relatives, parents or enemies, and not because they lack understanding or they have failed to put some principles in place. What an error! We should be promoting love and its fruits in the church, not anger, bitterness and fear. The true church, as Jesus Christ intended, was meant to encourage people to pursue God for themselves and live for their calling and life-purpose - this is what brings fulfilment in life.

2. Religiosity

Churches preach that prayer is the master key, so we took that on board in the singles group that I led, which was part of a fellowship group I attended regularly. We had prayer meetings every week, without fail. We quoted all manner of scriptures, cried out to God, declared and decreed. But after the meetings, I noticed that we all did nothing about acting on our faith. Life went on as normal. Of course some members were already active within their churches, going out for parties, trips, trying to meet people online, etc. but the majority of us never did. We thought that God would do a miracle and drop the husband at our door step. It never happened. When churches teach us to run after miracles, we cease to be real human beings i.e. thinking people! Tragic, isn't it?

> ***"Shallow men believe in luck and miracles but strong men believe in cause and effect"***
> – Ralph Waldo Emerson

Concerning the effort to achieve marriage via online dating, let me say this - hey, this is the twenty-first century, driven by advanced technology, so we may as well make use of it. If there are no social events where you live, meeting people online dating is not a bad idea, although you need guidance and wisdom in handling it. If you meet someone, try to meet in person too and get to know the real person. This call for maturity and emotional intelligence in order to avoid falling into the traps laid by the wrong people out there – so be warned.

Another key relating to religiosity is allowing church activities to steal away one's time and wider social life. You find that churches are using people for their own goals, then members are also using other members – resulting in slavery! I used to serve in almost every department, had choir practices that took almost the whole day every Saturday, spent Sunday morning in church and attended another fellowship in the afternoon. The week was always full of work, studies, mid-week church services and prayer meetings. So tell me, when would one get the time and opportunity to meet people? I used to think that since I was busy 'serving God', so God owed me a husband. I was wrong! Wake up my dear friend, and take back your time. Free yourself from church-slavery!

3. Lack of Initiative to Solve Social Problems (Egocentric churches)

Most of the AICs are aware of the rising number of single ladies in their churches, but do nothing about the problem. One common characteristic of such churches is that they are made up of small congregations (especially in the Western World). There are hardly any social events apart from church meetings and services. Even during these services, there are limited interactions. Immediately after the service, people just rush off to their families, work-shifts, and so on. No one is available, including Pastors! Everyone is 'facing their business'. Well, if we all just face 'our own business', then it shows that we have no principles guiding our lives; for example: the love principle would always push us to be a blessing to someone. The most common way for Pastors to show some concern was to raise a prayer point or two in one of the meetings.

Whilst living in Reading some years back, a friend of mine and I were attending different churches, and at one point, we came together to discuss a few issues about singleness. We both noticed that there were no Christian single people's events in Reading. She then came up with a very good suggestion, *"If churches really care about us (singles), they would do all they could to support us – like networking with all other local churches in town to organise joint socials where single people can meet each other."* Having been around AICs for years, I knew where the problem was – the churches were minding their own ego-centric business, others were competing with each other for increased numbers of membership, fearing that their members might decide to leave for other churches, and so on. Why wouldn't someone remain single in such circumstances?

4. Discrimination against women and unmarried ladies in ministry (surprisingly this does not apply to unmarried men!)

Esther Kuganja

I have previously been a very active church member. When one is single, because there is a desire to fill the void, one finds themselves serving in almost each and every church department: Bible Study Coordinator, Children's ministry, Choir, Intercessors group, Singles' groups, Pastor's Prayer Partners, …just name it, the singe ladies would be there!

I was involved in all that. After all, a single lady is free! And 'serving God' this way was believed to be good for her. However, I couldn't help noticing that there were roles I was not permitted to do e.g. leading congregational prayers or preaching. When ordaining ministers, unmarried brothers were ordained but no single sisters. I am still waiting for someone to give me a very good reason why. We stand against gender discrimination outside the church, what about within it?

As a single lady, you are never given a role of leadership in some churches. Why? Because 'you are not fit?' – Incapacitated because you are single! I stand against any church that has this attitude and does not believe in women leadership. Since Jesus Christ's mission on earth, we are under the dispensation of the Holy Spirit coming upon men and women who are ready for service and that God does not discriminate. He uses anyone who is willing and obedient. We should be careful when interpreting some texts in the Bible because if care is not taken, we could be copying a Jewish culture instead of the 'kingdom' culture.

"Be diligent to present yourself approved to God, a worker who does not need to be ashamed, rightly dividing the word of truth."
- 2 Timothy 2:15 (NKJV)

5. Racism (Oh, yes, this time among Africans)

Living in the Western world as an African, I naturally gravitated towards my kind. So the churches I found myself in were mostly African-dominated. And as if that was not enough, they also promoted the cultural background and beliefs of the pastor. For example if the Pastor was from Uganda, it would be the Ugandan way of doing things that was promoted and not a universal standard that encourages a more international congregation. It is sad.

The minority group in the church may begin to wonder, *"Do I really fit in here?"* This is because they feel alienated and ignored. At times people would speak and raise songs in their own dominant language, making others feel left out. So when the minority don't want to be seen as unfriendly, they are forced to learn the songs in order to be able to fit in. Whatever happened to the universal language? No wonder, majority of AICs are not popular at community outreaches in the Western world. We should be promoting the kingdom culture in our churches, and not any other.

What explains the significant numbers of single unmarried ladies in churches today? I can say that there are fewer church-going men. And for most AICs that I was acquainted with, I could not help but notice that although people gathered from different nationalities, still most members tended to marry from their countries of origin; even to the extent of going back to Africa to get a wife or meet someone online, but not from the church itself. Could there be trust issues? Such a mentality keeps single ladies on the shelf and as if that is not tiring enough, the weekly or monthly deliverance services (with hardly any fruit), are exhausting too.

6. Negative attitudes

My friends, this book is about reality. This is why I have used most of my experiences to bring out the message. I would like to show you below some of the statements that were made regarding my single status by people I know very well:

a) *"Where is your God? Why isn't God answering your prayers?"*

Let God be God, He alone knows what we don't. Let us not assume that because one is single, then the only prayer on their mind is, *"Lord, give me a husband!"* There are so many other discussions we hold with God on a personal level.

b) *"You should start wearing bright colours and clothes that are tight on you."*

Whilst I do understand that it is important for one to always be presentable, having such statements thrown at you can be so degrading. Where is respect and acceptance for one another?

c) *"My sister, it is because of unforgiveness - do not let the root of bitterness remain in you."*

Since when have people become so discerning, as to know what is in my heart? Friends, let us not use other people's 'tragedies' to judge them, but instead offer acceptance, love and protection to them.

d) *"Pray my sister; it seems you are not praying enough."*

So when is prayer actually enough? Till am blue in the face and have no strength left in me?

e) *"You have been a good Christian, kept yourself pure, and yet God is not answering your prayers. There must be something wrong with you."*

Well, let God speak for himself. Even Job, a biblical figure was accused by friends of having sinned, yet God just allowed the events in his life for a purpose.

f) *"I am sending you links to a series of messages on witchcraft, which I thought may bless you."*

This was part of an email I received in October, 2016. It was very thoughtful of the sender, but no thanks! What made her think that I was interested in such messages? In fact, this was a surprise email after a long period of not being in touch with the person. Let us always bear in mind, that the way we last saw a person years ago, is certainly not the same way they currently are. This is because time is a function of change - in character, personal values and choices, etc. So a lot could have happened in that time that negates our judgements. Let us be careful in this aspect when relating to people – this wisdom could save many relationships and friendships in the future.

> *"We are not put on this earth to see through one another but to see one another through."*
> – Peter de Vries

7. Lack of genuine love

I was amazed that it was considered normal and okay for pastors and men in the church not to give single ladies a simple brotherly hug. Why? Because you are single! Married men rarely accepted any fellowship invitations from unmarried women, nor could they invite them to their homes. This is considered taboo: *"What if I develop feelings for her?"* or *"People may think we are having an affair."* Well, I know the main reason here is self-preservation but such men are only protecting their own 'demons' that they have not dealt with yet! This is a fact.

> **"Sometimes the church talks about singleness as if it were similar to being chosen for 'Hufflepuff' by the Magic Sorting Hat in Harry Potter. The good news is that you still are at Hogwarts, but the bad news is that pretty much everyone else there will avoid you and makes it clear they feel sad for you and would never, ever want to be you."**
> - Sammy Rhodes

Thanks to the mentorship of Dr. Sunday Adelaja, I have learned that men are put there to reveal the love of God to the women around them. They are supposed to show courtesy to all women around them, not just their wives. This is when they are called 'gentlemen' - simple courtesy without feelings! This is a concept of love that is universal, available for everyone. Love is not egocentric – it should not only be shown to one's spouse or family - what about other people? The goal of fellowship is to make everyone feel accepted and loved. Faith in God alone does not guarantee you for heaven. It has to be complimented by *universal love*.

The church should work to make sure that the interest of members are paramount, putting their interest above that of the church. Where churches are run by egocentric leaders is a sign of a lack of value systems and love! The members of the church are our neighbours, who are supposed to experience this love first. The church should be a place where we experience love and encouragement, instead we sense rejection, suppression and are discriminated against. No wonder ladies walk out to look for love in the wrong places. Let's change the way we do church folks!

> *"Beloved, let us love one another, for love is of God; and everyone who loves is born of God and knows God."*
> – 1 John 4:7 NKJV

I hope that by now you have an idea of the 'drama' in churches and what limits the growth and potential of unmarried ladies. Negative stereotypes need to be stamped out in order to make the whole environment healthier and more loving for everyone. In the next chapter, we are going to look at some facts that explain why there are high numbers of single people today. This will help us appreciate the problem and not jump to conclusions about unmarried people. It is my desire that you will find the chapter informative.

Character Aroma Nuggets Part 4:

1) Everything happens for a purpose – Anon
2) *"To handle yourself, use your head; to handle others, use your heart."* – J. John
3) *"'Be still, and know that I am God; I will be exalted among the nations, I will be exalted in the earth."* - Psalm 46:10 (NKJV)
4) You are not tied down to a particular church so have the liberty to step out if you do not agree with some things.
5) Develop an intimate relationship with your creator through regular personal retreats. Learn to be guided by him and not to depend on a pastor – he's just a man.
6) *"Never be in a hurry to judge people because you have not been through what they have gone through and have not been tested the way they are tested."* – Dr. Sunday Adelaja
7) Keep your distance from negativity. It pollutes the mind and hinders progress in one's life.
8) *"You shall love the Lord your God with all your heart, with all your soul, and with all your mind.' This is the first and great commandment. And the second is like it: 'You shall love your neighbor as yourself,"* Matthew 22:37-39 (NKJV)
9) Establish boundaries in your life: Know which are your 'no-go' places, people or doctrines. This is because environment is a major factor to our success in life.
10) *"The greatest happiness of life is the conviction that we are loved; loved for ourselves, or rather loved in spite of ourselves."* – Victor Hugo

Recall and Deliberate (Part 4)

<u>To the General Reader</u>

a) What kind of doctrines are taught and upheld in your church? Do they proclaim an abused gospel (that of curses and demons) or the true gospel (that of repentance, restitution, love and being our brother's keeper)?
b) Is your church pre-occupied with tithes and offering without paying attention to the individual lives of the people and addressing their needs?
c) As a leader or Pastor, how much of knowledge and strategies do you have to help your members solve their problems?
d) Have you taken note that women can also hold major ministerial positions in a church and so should be encouraged to do so? Do you understand that in the sight of God men and women are equal?
e) What are your thoughts on inter-cultural or ethnic marriages? As Christians should we be limited to marriage that is only within an ethnic or cultural group or a nation?
f) How do you understand God's love? In showing it, are we restricted to a selected few or to all including single sisters?

<u>To the Stigmatized Single Lady</u>

You need to find value in yourself. You need to understand that you are worthy. You need to have an understanding that the fact that you are still single doesn't make you a less human being and so feel dejected. Rather, you must understand that the right person hasn't found you yet. Those who have been ignoring you are not for you. The one for you will find you irresistible. You are a princess! You are a jewel in the eyes of God. So, concentrate

Esther Kuganja

on being a right wife material and fulfill your own life purpose. As regards the right person, he will come most times at the least expected. Wait till the right time. It won't tarry!

Chapter 5

Facing the Brutal Facts

Why do We Have Many Single People in Our Societies Today?

"There is no transformation of life without the renewing of the mind."
Dr. Sunday Adelaja

The aim of this chapter is to bring out life situations, reasons or facts that explain why there are many more unwed men and women in our societies all over the world compared to years back. I call them brutal facts because they can be the kind that we do not normally want to acknowledge. They can be painful both to the affected individual and to society as a whole. Some of these reasons are from my own experience; some from the experiences of other single ladies that I know or have read about, so I hope this chapter will be an eye-opener to help you understand singleness from a new perspective.

In America for example, women make up more than half of the unmarried population. There are a hundred single women to eighty-eight unmarried men[11]. That is a significant gap. There are a number of reasons why people remain single. Let us explore some of them below:

1. **Failed Relationships**

   For some women, there may have been opportunities for marriage, but things just did not work out. Disappointment sets in and may blind and shield them from other marriage prospects. This is mainly because such people no longer trust themselves or others.

2. **Desperation**

   I have known of ladies who out of desperation hop from train to train, bus to bus, church to church, conference to conference, … you name it, in order to somehow bump into 'Mr. Right' but nothing happens. In some cases, something did happen but it was an 'accident' – oops! A Mr. Wrong! Desperation can be written all over a lady's face, and show up in her mannerisms, to the extent that it puts men off. And can make a woman to be vulnerable to various forms of manipulation. Desperation rarely attracts positivity in life, because it promotes a 'short-cut' kind of mentality, which overlooks the necessity of processing principles that can birth better results.

3. **Fulfilment Outside Marriage**

   Some people want to follow celibacy. If marriage is a source of fulfilment, why do we have happy celibate people, high rates of separation and divorce and some parents in pain caused by their children? I have heard people confess that the deepest pain in their lives was caused by either their spouses or children. Others agree that they actually lost their calling and purpose in life whilst married. Hey… single ladies, have some pride in your status!

4. Lack of Social Engagements and Busy Routines

The lonely and busy lifestyle of the west can get so isolating. One may have no social exposure unless they intentionally make efforts. This is because after a really long day, the only thing that comes to mind is your bed, not an evening out. And for some ladies, there is a tendency to retreat to one's shell. They would rather avoid social events all together, because such events remind them who they are – everybody else is coupled-up!

5. The Man Deficit

The shortage of men is a reality in some communities. Fascinating, isn't it? In most AICs, the ratio of men to women in churches is as little as one to six. We do not need an official survey here. Any regular church-goer will agree with me that women are the most dominant. Where are the men? And what are churches doing about this? This is a clear challenge for Christians to evangelise men.

In 1948, Alfred Kinsey, author of *Sexual Behaviour in the Human Male*, shocked the world by announcing that ten percent of the male population was gay[12]. This may be higher since the legalisation of gay marriage. Another research by Jon Birger[13] revealed that there are five women to every four men among college graduates in America. He reports that in New York City, nine to twelve percent of men are gay – this reduces the number of heterosexual men available.

6. World Standards of an 'Ideal' Woman

When all the media paints the picture of the 'right' body size and shape, fashion sense, make-up and all that stuff, single ladies are faced with two options - conform totally or compete. Don't get me wrong dear friend, it's okay to do the things that enhance our beauty, but problems arise when such things get us 'enslaved' to the extent of losing our own identity. These days, marriages in our societies are driven by materialism and physical appearance, and not by who people are on the inside and their value system.

7. Allegiance to Popular Beliefs and Own Culture

It is commonly believed that marrying a person from a similar cultural background is advantageous – I agree a hundred percent. But in some cases, this may not be realistic. For example: people migrate to different nations for various reasons and they may find themselves in an area with people from various nationalities. So do Ugandans, for example, need to go back to Uganda to find a spouse? Anyone with such a mentality obviously lacks a genuine love for others. They are assuming that their own culture is superior or may be thinking, "What will my family think of me marrying from outside my tribe or nationality?" Such stereotypes leave many ladies unmarried. In AICs, there is a lack of emphasis on the practicality of Christian principles or kingdom values such as love for people and seeing everyone as a special person made in the image of God and worthy of love, honour, respect and acceptance. Instead, these same churches are promoting man-made cultures and traditions. This is sad.

8. **Self-pity and a 'Victim' Mentality**

When we entertain self-pity, we are shielded from the current reality. What goes on inside of us becomes our present reality. There should be a check in place. Whenever you sense such a state, switch your mind to focus on your past victories, on words, music or personalities who inspire you. This will help you to escape.

> *"Self-pity is easily the most destructive of the non-pharmaceutical narcotics; it is addictive, gives momentary pleasure and separates the victim from reality."*
> - John Gardner

Having a victim's mentality used to be my major problem. I blamed circumstances, my looks, my parents and anyone else I could find. The truth is – I was in error! To make matters worse, the so-called men of God would make you believe that others do not want you to be happy, so they could have indulged in some form of witchcraft to ensure that you had no happiness. I now see all this as nonsense! Even if it were true, once you know who you are, whose you are and what you have inside of you, nothing can stop your joy, not even Satan himself!

> ***"You are of God, little children, and have overcome them, because He who is in you is greater than he who is in the world."***
> 1 John 4:4 NKJV

9. Strong Family Ties

Some cultures, especially Asian, can be actively involved in the marital settlement of their children. As a result such people get married earlier in life or need to wait for an arranged marriage.

10. Fear of Taking Risks and Commitment

Marriage can be likened to gambling – you never know for sure what you're going to get. The media is busy throwing all kinds of negativity in our faces – divorce rates, domestic abuse, homicide, greed, control, etc. These can discourage many people from making a commitment because no one wants to get hurt. Besides, there are few role models to portray the ideal picture of a godly marriage, full of friendship, genuine love and forbearance. Please note that there are some success stories that should act as a source of encouragement, if we choose to pay attention to them and seek to develop the principles being practiced in our own lives.

11. Past Wounds and Behavioural Patterns

A number of single ladies have had relationships in the past, but due to internal and external factors they were not able to maintain those relationships. These factors could range from trust and anger issues, dominance, hygiene problems, and so on. I would advise that anyone with such problems should seek professional help from counsellors. My other advice would be not to bring the hurts of a past relationship into the new one.

As a defence mechanism, some people choose celibacy to avoid getting hurt again. Others may have recently broken up and don't want to start a new relationship on the rebound. Events in our childhood play a big role - if your childhood was not full of parental love, security and trust, you may end up with a negative attitude, insecurity, low self-esteem, distrust and so on, which could have the result of trapping you into singleness.

12. Other Priorities like Career, Travel or Personal Dreams

Although some ladies would like to get married, they may not be willing to give up their dreams. It is generally believed that marriage is a very old tradition and people of a conservative nature may become trapped in it. Some men are simply not emotionally available; they are busy focussing on 'making it in life' and may have other means of fulfilling their sexual desires.

13. Many would like to retain their independence

One of the basic human needs is security, and if marriage these days does not seem to offer that, people would prefer to remain independent.

> ***"Don't be fretting... about me marrying. Marrying's a trouble and not marrying's a trouble and I stick to the trouble I know."***
> - L.M. Montgomery

14. Less Marriage-material Men out there

At one point in time, my single friends and I discussed our predicament: *"There are no more nice men out there; they have all been taken."* We had experiences of some men approaching us but even the approach itself scored low. They were too lazy to learn how to do things right. There were cases of men who lived double lives – having a wife back in Africa, and wanting another abroad. Some men could be chasing two or three ladies at the same time, while others showed no sign of courtesy to a lady, no values, etc. They seem to just want one thing – sex. You could read it on their faces! A total put-off!

I do understand when people believe the problem is not about the scarcity of men, but rather that the ones available who are not 'real men'. By real men here, I am referring to those who are responsible (with evidence), have goals and are ready to be fathers. What some ladies see around them are 'boys' looking for 'mothers' to solve their emotional, financial and immigration status issues. No, thank you!

15. Being Picky

Throughout my experience of interacting with single people who have turned down a prospective relationship, I have heard reasons like: *"I do not trust people of this nationality," "too dark," "has a history," "too short," "has no College degree," "looks cheap," "does he genuinely love me, or just want a marriage of convenience?" "has children,"* and so on.

> **"Our own defenses often leave us feeling pickier and more judgmental. This is particularly true after we've had bad experiences, where we were deceived or rejected by a person for whom we had strong feelings."**[14]
> - Dr. Lisa Firestone

While I do understand the need to be cautious of people approaching you for marriage, extreme pickiness can be a disaster. Let us always remember that we marry 'potential' not 'perfection'. Just like raw materials are transformed into the desired finished product, one has a job to do in their chosen partner's life. This is the main reason why marriage is only for 'mature' people!

Well, we have come to the end of this chapter where we have discussed the various reasons that force people to remain single. The list is not exhaustive but it gives you an idea of the reality of our world. I hope you can have an informed and balanced view about single people. In the next chapter, we are going to look at examples of people who made it through life and left a mark in history despite being single. Now that is interesting!

Character Aroma Nuggets Part 5:

1) *"Not forgiving someone is like drinking poison expecting the other person to die."* – Anon
2) Love is not just a feeling, but a choice; give people the freedom to choose for themselves.
3) Mutual respect and honour is the key to laying a strong foundation for a successful marriage.
4) *"Be willing to step outside your comfort zone once in a while; take the risks in life that seem worth taking. The ride might not be as predictable as if you'd just planted your feet and stayed put, but it will be a heck of a lot more interesting."* - Edward Whitacre, Jr
5) Resolve some major issues before commitment: background, temperament, education, religion, family, sexuality, finances, communication, health and others.
6) *"Those who don't want to take risks in life end up being the losers."* - Dr Sunday Adelaja
7) Because of our negative past experiences, many of us continue to carry emotional baggage. This can be a form of 'sickness – being emotionally unwell. It is not a curse or demon as some can make you believe. These are simply behavioural patterns that have developed overtime through experiences in life. It is advisable to seek professional help from psychologists or other trained personnel to help you overcome the problem.
8) *"We all carry flaws and these vulnerabilities are especially apparent when getting close to one another. Thus, achieving intimacy is a brave battle, but it is one well-worth fighting for, each and every day, both within ourselves and, ultimately, within our relationships."* - Dr. Lisa Firestone
9) When we remain truthful, guided by our own personal values, and being open to love, then we

stand a greater chance of finding that authentic relationship that leads to marriage.
10) *"Delay is often just the protective hand of a loving Father"* – Dr. Creflo Dollar

Recall and deliberate (Part 5)

<u>To the General Reader:</u>

- a) As a reader of this book, do you know of any other reasons why we have many single ladies in our society?
- b) How many desperate singles have you personally shown love, guidance or encouragement to?
- c) If a single is enjoying his or her celibacy regardless of their age, why is there a need to convince him or her into marriage?
- d) In what ways can you create opportunities for singles to mingle?
- e) How can we bring singles together using their areas of interest as it seems some may be looking out for someone with whom they share similar passions?
- f) What ways can we challenge the societal standard of an "ideal woman"?
- g) Are you an advocate of strong family ties? How else do you want singles to find their soul mates?
- h) For the men, in what ways can you model authentic manhood in the home and society so that other single men and youngsters can imitate?

<u>To the Stigmatized Single Lady</u>

You must be fully aware that you are a master of your own thoughts and decisions. As a Christian single your purpose in life is your priority and you have a right to protect it by the choice(s) you make. If you so desire to be single then don't allow anyone override your status after all, it is your life and you must account for it. However, if you still desire to be married, then follow your passions by being with those who share the same passions as you are. It means you have to be selective of the groups or environments you spend time with. Don't also shut out social media or Christian online meeting sites, but you must be wise and connect with genuine people. By their fruits you shall always know them.

Chapter 6

Examples of Great Achievers Despite Singleness

Let Nothing Stop You from Becoming an Achiever

"Don't ignore the love you do have in your life by focusing on the love you don't."
Mandy Hale

One may ask, "Can I really make it as a single lady in this world of negative stereotypes?" The aim of this chapter is to answer that question as well as to bring hope and faith to many lives out there. If you are a single person, just know that you are not alone. Mandy Hale (2013) said, "*Hope for love, pray for love, wish for love, dream for love... but don't put your life on hold waiting for love.*" It is possible to live a fulfilled life and become an achiever despite singleness.

This chapter outlines forty different personalities who did just that! There are more people out there but I have listed just forty of them because this book marks my fortieth birthday. I hope, dear friend, that you will find this chapter enlightening and that it will get you fired up to make a contribution to your generation.

1) Joan of Arc (1412-1431), is considered a heroine of France for her role during the Lancastrian phase

of the Hundred Years' War, and was canonized as a Roman Catholic saint. Despite her age and gender, she courageously led the French army to recover France from English domination and gained prominence.

2) Leonardo da Vinci (1452-1519), a famous Italian often referred to the father of paleontology, ichnology, and architecture. He is considered one of the greatest painters in history.

3) Queen Elizabeth I (1533-1603) was the Queen of England and Ireland from 1558 till her death. She is referred to as *The Virgin Queen*.

> **"I would rather be a beggar and single than a queen and married."**

4) René Descartes (1596-1650) was a French philosopher, mathematician and scientist. He is recognised as the father of analytical geometry and a key figure in the scientific revolution.

5) Sir Isaac Newton (1642-1727) was an English physicist and mathematician, widely recognized as one of the most influential scientists of all time and a key figure in the scientific revolution.

6) Antonio Vivaldi (1678-1741) was an Italian composer, violinist, teacher and cleric. He is recognized as one of the greatest Baroque composers – whose work included: instrumental concertos, sacred choral works and more than forty operas. His most famous piece is *The Four Seasons*.

7) François-Marie Arouet (1694-1778) was a French writer, historian, and philosopher famous for his humour and his attacks on the established Catholic Church. He advocated freedom of religion, speech, and the separation of church and state. Voltaire produced plays, poems, novels, essays and historical and scientific works. He used his works to criticize intolerance and religious dogma.

8) Ludwig van Beethoven (1770-1827) was a famous German and influential composer and pianist. He played a key role during the transition between the Classical and Romantic eras in Western art music. His compositions include: 9 symphonies, 5 piano concertos, 1 violin concerto, 32 piano sonatas, 16 string quartets, his great Mass - *the Missa solemnis*, and one opera, *Fidelio*.

"I love a tree more than a man."[15]

9) Meriwether Lewis (1774-1809) was an American explorer, soldier, politician, and public administrator. He led the exploration into the territory of the Louisiana Purchase and also collected scientific data and information on aboriginals. He was appointed Governor of Upper Louisiana in 1806 by President Thomas Jefferson.
10) Jane Austen (1775-1817) was an English novelist whose work highlighted women's pursuit of social status and economic security through the dependence on marriage. In her letter to her niece Fanny Knight, dated November 18, 1814, Jane stated:

"Anything is to be preferred and endured rather than marrying without affection."[16]

11) President James Buchanan (1791-1868) served as the 15th President of the United States from 1857 to 1861. Having served in the United States House of Representatives and the Senate, he became the Minister to Russia under President Andrew Jackson and later Secretary of State under President James K. Polk. As of 2016, he is the last former Secretary of State to serve as President of the United States. He was appointed Ambassador to the United Kingdom by President Franklin Pierce and helped draft the Ostend Manifesto.

12) Hans Christian Anderson (1805-1875) was a Danish author best remembered for his fairy tales for children that presented lessons of virtue and resilience in times of challenges; suitable for adults too.
13) Henry David Thoreau (1817-1862) was an American essayist, poet, philosopher, abolitionist, naturalist, tax resister, development critic, surveyor, and historian. He is best known for his book "Walden - a reflection upon simple living in natural surroundings", and his essay "Civil Disobedience" - an argument for disobedience to an unjust state.

> **"I never found the companion that was so companionable as solitude."**[17]

14) Anne Brontë (1820-1849) was an English novelist and poet. Her works included: *Agnes Grey*, a novel based upon her experiences as a governess and *The Tenant of Wildfell Hall*, which is considered to be one of the first feminist novels.
15) Susan Brownell Anthony (1820-1906), a social reformer and women's rights advocate who pioneered the women's suffrage movement in America. When asked about her marital status, these were her responses:

> **"It always happened that the men I wanted were those I could not get, and those who wanted me I wouldn't have."**[18]

> **"I never found the man who was necessary to my happiness. I was very well as I was."**[19]

> **"I never felt I could give up my life of freedom to become a man's housekeeper. When I was young, if a girl married poor, she became a housekeeper and a drudge. If she married wealth she became a pet**

and a doll. Just think, had I married at twenty, I would have been a drudge or a doll for fifty-nine years. Think of it!"[20]

16) Florence Nightingale (1820-1910) was an English social reformer and statistician, and the founder of modern nursing. She gave up her prospects for marriage and a comfortable life just to heal the sick and take care of wounded soldiers during the Crimean War. This is because in her day, men were very controlling of their wives. She believed that one passion would kill another. Her passion was to care for the sick and poor in society. She was nick-named 'The Lady with the Lamp'. Hospital designers would ask for her advice. In 1860, she established the Nightingale Training School for nurses at St. Thomas's Hospital in London. All over Britain, the nursing training was established on the Nightingale model.

17) Elizabeth Blackwell (1821-1910) was a women rights activist and the first female physician in US. She was an active social reformer and author.

"My mind is fully made up. I have not the slightest hesitation on the subject; the thorough study of medicine, I am quite resolved to go through with. The horrors and disgusts I have no doubt of vanquishing. I have overcome stronger distastes than any that now remain, and feel fully equal to the contest. As to the opinion of people, I don't care one straw personally; though I take so much pains, as a matter of policy, to propitiate it, and shall always strive to do so; for I see continually how the highest good is eclipsed by the violent or disagreeable forms which contain it."[21]

18) Clara Barton (1821-1912) was a teacher, patent clerk and a pioneering nurse who founded the American Red Cross. Her humanitarian work at a time when relatively few women worked outside the home was remarkable.
19) Louisa May Alcott (1832-1888) was an American novelist and poet, who grew up among well-known intellectuals of her days like Ralph Waldo Emerson, Nathaniel Hawthorne and Henry David Thoreau. Her famous novels include: Little Women (1868), Little Men (1871) and Jo's Boys (1886).[22]
20) Charlotte Digges Moon (1840-1912) was a hard-working missionary in China for almost forty years. It is thanks to her work as a teacher and evangelist that support for missions among the American Baptists was established.
21) Mary Stevenson Cassatt (1844-1926) was an American painter and printmaker. Her creative pieces depicted images of the social and private lives of women, especially the relationships between mothers and their children.

"I am independent! I can live alone and I love to work."[23]

22) George Eastman (1854-1932) was an American innovator and entrepreneur who founded the Eastman Kodak Company that played a pivotal role in the invention of motion picture film in 1888 by the world's first film-makers Eadweard Muybridge and Louis Le Prince. He was a major philanthropist for higher education institutions and also funded clinics in London and other European cities to serve low-income residents.
23) Nikola Tesla (1856-1943) a Serbian-American engineer and physicist best known for his contributions to the design of the modern alternating current electricity supply system.[24]

How a Single Woman Can Overcome Stigmatisation

> ***"I do not think there is any thrill that can go through the human heart like that felt by the inventor... such emotions make a man forget food, sleep, friends, love, everything."***[25]

24) Jane Addams (1860-1935) was an American reformer, social worker, philosopher, author and leader in women's suffrage and world peace. She was a role model for middle-class women who desired to improve their communities. Jane was the first American woman to be awarded the Nobel Peace Prize in 1931. She is remembered as the founder of the social work profession in US.
25) The Wright Brothers, Wilbur (1867-1912) and Orville (1871-1948), were two American brothers who are generally credited with inventing, building, and flying the world's first successful aeroplane.
26) Helen Adams Keller (1880-1968) was an American author, political activist, and lecturer. She campaigned for women's suffrage, labor rights and socialism. Helen is recognised as the first deaf-blind person to be awarded a Bachelor of Arts degree. The *Helen Keller Day* is celebrated in Pennsylvania on her birthday.
27) Gabrielle Bonheur Chanel (1883-1971) was a French legendary clothing designer and businesswoman who founded the Chanel brand. Lady Chanel was the only fashion designer to first appear on Time Magazine's "Most Influential People of the twentieth century."
28) Franz Kafka (1883-1924) is considered as one of the most influential writers of the twentieth century. Some of his famous works include: *The Metamorphosis, The Trial,* and *The Castle*. The term *Kafkaesque* is now part of the English language, describing situations like those in his writings.[26]

29) Greta Garbo (1905-1990), was a Swedish-born American film actress. In 1999 she was ranked fifth female star of Classic Hollywood Cinema by the American Film Institute. She chose to concentrate on her career and turned down numerous marriage proposals which was taboo at the time.

> ***"If you are blessed you are blessed, whether you are married or single."***

> ***"I never said, 'I want to be alone.' I only said, 'I want to be left alone!' There is all the difference."***

> ***"There are some who want to get married and others who don't. I have never had an impulse to go to the altar. I am a difficult person to lead."*** [27]

30) Mother Theresa (1910–1997) was a Roman Catholic nun who devoted her life to serving the poor and destitute around the world. She spent many years in Calcutta, India where she founded the Missionaries of Charity, a religious congregation devoted to helping those in great need. In 1979, Mother Teresa was awarded the Nobel Peace Prize and has become a symbol of charitable selfless work. She was canonised as a saint by the Roman Catholic Church in 2016.[28]

31) Nelle Harper Lee (1926-2016), was an American writer, famous for the novel *To Kill a Mockingbird* that won her the Pulitzer Prize. In 2007, she was awarded the Presidential Medal of Freedom for her contribution to literature.[29]

32) Gloria Marie Steinem (1934 - now) is an American journalist and social and political activist. She supported the feminist movement saying things like, *"The surest way to be alone is to get married."* Then, after she had done everything one could

How a Single Woman Can Overcome Stigmatisation

hope to do in a lifetime, she fell in love. She got married at the age of sixty-six and made no apologies[30].

33) Diane Keaton (1946 - now) is an American film actress, director and producer. Her films have earned her over US$1.1 billion in North America.

"I didn't really want a man that I could have. The dream or the neighbourhood? I wanted the dream. I remember when I was young I honestly believed in some ridiculous way that you would find someone who would be the person you lived with until you died. I don't think that because I'm not married it's made my life any less. That old maid myth is garbage."[31]

34) Oprah Winfrey (1954 - now) is famously known for her talk show: The Oprah Winfrey Show. She is well known as 'Queen of All Media', the greatest black philanthropist and is currently North America's first and only multi-billionaire black person and the most influential woman in the world.

"I think that had Stedman and I gotten married, we certainly wouldn't have stayed married... The show was the true love of my life - it took up all of my energy."[32]

35) Condoleezza Rice (1954 - now) is an American political scientist and diplomat. She served as the sixty-sixth United States Secretary of State - the first female African-American Secretary of State, the second African-American Secretary of State (after Colin Powell) and the second female Secretary of State (after Madeleine Albright).

36) Susan Magdalane Boyle (1961- now) is a Scottish singer, one of Britain's best-selling artists who confessed at the age of fifty, that she has never

been kissed! She is famous for the '*I Dreamed a Dream*' performance on Britain's Got Talent in 2009.

"I live by myself with my cat Pebbles... but I have the support of all my brothers and sisters and my neighbours and friends."[33]

37) Kristin Davis (1965 - now) is another famous American actress and producer. She pursued her dream of becoming an actress from the age of nine. Davis has been a Global Ambassador for Oxfam since 2004, travelling to support their work in Haiti, Mozambique, and South Africa.[34]

"I'm perfectly happy with my single self."[35]

38) Rev Dr. Kate Coleman (1964 - now) is one of Britain's most influential black Christian women. She is founding director of Next Leadership. She has nearly 30 years of leadership experience in the church, charity and voluntary sectors and is a mentor and coach to leaders. Kate recently completed a term as Chair of the Evangelical Alliance Council (2012-2014), is a former president of the Baptist Union of Great Britain (2006-2007), and a Baptist Minister. A popular speaker and lecturer, Kate has gained a reputation as a visionary and an inspiration to many. She is a strategic advisor who mentors, coaches and supports leaders and organisations locally, nationally and internationally. Her network extends across all sectors and church denominations. Kate is author of the book: *7 Deadly Sins of Women in Leadership*. Her media contributions include the mainstream press, radio and TV. Kate is a Certified Stakeholder Centered Coach.[36]

39) Chelsea Joy Handler (1975 - now) is an American comedian, actress, writer, television host and

producer. New York's *Time* magazine placed her among the top 100 Most Influential People in 2012.[37]

"I don't know that I'm marriage material."[38]

40) Charlize Theron (1975 - now) is a South African and American actress and film producer. She adopted two children on her own and proved that anyone can create their own happiness.

"I like the fact that I'm single at thirty-eight. That's not necessarily what a lot of women want ... but I'm just saying, a life is good if it's the life that you want....I am living my life in a way that if tomorrow it ended and I hope not because I have a kid—but if it did, this was the life that I really wanted to live. But I work at that, you know?"[39]

People always assume that if a lady is single and especially; if aged thirty-five and over, then they are unhappy with their lives. I hope that this chapter will change that view and show the masses that it is possible to be satisfied and fulfilled living an enjoyable single life. My question here is, *"What are you doing with your life – single or married?"*

Character Aroma Nuggets Part 6:

1) *"You don't need anyone but yourself to live an incredible life and have people remember you long after you're gone"* - Samara O'Shea
2) All the personalities mentioned in this chapter became great because they chose to focus on their passion and the life that they wanted to live rather than on public opinion.
3) Knowing one's capabilities is crucial to making the decision whether or not to marry.
4) People have come and gone, and you are not an exception. But just ask yourself this one thing: "What will I be remembered for?"
5) It's never too late to put your life in order – there is another chance as long as you still have breath.
6) There is a purpose behind every problem. In trying to solve the problem, we undergo processes that birth in us qualities which were hidden within. We then become experts.
7) You are unique and nobody can ever be you. That is why your assignment is specific to you.
8) We serve God by serving others; we love God by loving others.
9) Living for a purpose should be the only way to live.
10) *"Your equipping often takes place in the process of fulfilling your assignment."* – Bob Gass

Recall and Deliberate (Part 6)

<u>To the General Reader</u>

a) What is it that you are living for – life purpose, the belly, the money or the sexual satisfaction?
b) Has there been a time when you woke up to the reality that life should be more than this?
c) Take an inventory of your life, what is it worth if you are to weigh it in terms of living for yourself or for a course?
d) After reading this chapter, what are you going to do about your life?
e) Would you dust that project that has been lying aimlessly on your shelf and get off to work?

<u>To the Stigmatized Single Lady</u>

What has been your resolve after reading this chapter? Are you going to let society continue to weigh you down or are you going to take the 'bull by the horns', fulfilling your passions or achieving your purpose? It is time to brace up my friend! Man up to the whole life ahead of you. There is more to life than you can ever imagine, only change your thinking.

Chapter 7

The Journey of Self-discovery

Discover the Treasure in You First, and then Others Will See it Too

> *"Your time is limited, so don't waste it by living someone else's life. Don't be trapped by dogmas which are only a result of other people's thinking. Don't let the noise of other opinions muffle your own inner voice. The most important thing is to have the courage to follow your heart and intuition. Somehow, they already know what you truly want to become. Everything else is secondary."*
> Steve Jobs

The achievers we just looked at in the previous chapter could not have made it if they had not discovered who they were. Self-discovery is a very important journey. This chapter is unique because in it I share with you how I changed my self-perception and worked on my weaknesses; the process I went through to examine my current state and what I wanted to become. Outlined in this chapter are some bold steps to help anyone resist the negativity from both internal and external sources. I trust this journey will help many people to discover who they are and why they are here on planet earth.

a) Dealing with the Internal Issues

When I reflect back on my life, my main struggles were anger and insecurity which could have come from the constant criticism that I received whilst growing up. I hardly remember any birthday celebrations for me and I could recall few really joyful events in my life. I had to struggle hard to get anything good, nothing came to me easily. I was a quiet and reserved person and grew up with so much bitterness in me. With few friends and poor social skills, that 'angry' little girl was still living in my adult body! I had to totally forgive and put behind me all the anger I felt towards parents, siblings, teachers, colleagues or relatives who caused one form of damage or the other in my life. I suggest that anyone going through such things as I did should open up to a mother-figure or psychologist who can help.

Recognise your limitations and weaknesses and commit yourself to managing them e.g. if you have a weakness in the area of pornography, avoid the internet, films and magazines that feed that weakness especially when alone. If you enjoy gossip, change the company of friends that feed this weakness – let your words be always aimed at building not tearing, healing not destroying; mind your own business!

b) Becoming the 'architect' of your own life

Other problems I had were a poor self-image, lack of confidence and an inferiority complex. I never thought I was beautiful; nobody ever told me so – I saw myself as too fat, too short, too dark, and so on. I believed that this could have been the reason why men never approached me. I needed to fall in love with who I was – with my personality. In September 2009, I heard of a Conference led by Reverend Joe Olaiya of Living Faith Foundation. I decided to attend and during one of the sessions we were taught about the significance of one's names. When

I discovered the meaning of my names as they were then, I was not comfortable with them anymore. My first name, Mary, means 'bitter' and the surname Namuyanja means 'woman of the sea' (in my native language). After the conference, I gave my next step some thought, even talked to my father about it, and also sought counsel from elderly people I respected.

Two months later, I changed my names to Esther Kuganja. I love my current names. Esther means 'star' and besides, I felt a calling towards my people in Uganda and Africa as a whole, which was similar to the call of Queen Esther as recorded in the Bible. The surname: Kuganja means 'favour or mercy'. I love this portion of Psalm 23: '*goodness and mercy to follow me all the days of my life*'. The name change helped me to feel more positive about myself, and this attracted more positivity in my life too. Please note that name-changing is not for everyone! This was just my way of dealing with some internal battles in my life then. For other people, different options could be employed.

I also learnt to speak words of peace, life, acceptance, faith and hope to myself, oh yes, have some good self-talk! This helped to boost my confidence. I no longer had to wait for somebody to make me happy; I learnt to make myself happy and fulfilled by enjoying the things I love to do – solitude, travelling, jogging, investing in my career, reading, fellowshipping, eating out with friends or by myself. I learnt to enjoy my own company (we all need this). And of course, a close relationship with God made me joyful no matter the situation. I knew beyond any reasonable doubt that I was never alone.

> *"I never feel alone realizing the fact that my life is my only life partner"*
> - Munia Khan

c) Adding value to yourself

Life is all about adding value to yourself. In pursuit of knowledge, I enrolled at the History Makers' Bible School, London between the year 2010 and 2011. This helped to expand my understanding of my life's purpose and calling. My knowledge of the Bible and Christian faith increased. I could identify wrong doctrines much more easily than previously. I learnt the importance of monthly solitude mainly for rest, prayer, self-evaluation or reading. Immediately after the end of my course, I enrolled for the Oak Seed Executive Leadership Course at the Institute for National Transformation, London between the year 2011 and 2012). During this time, I learnt to challenge myself to grow by regular reading and study. I started getting involved with different charity organisations in Reading with the aim of helping them to achieve a higher performance. It was during this time that the burden for Africa in my heart became even stronger, and the Character Aroma Project, a Non-governmental Organisation based in Uganda, was birthed. The aim of this organisation is to transform Ugandan life through raising leaders of character.

Other areas of self-development include self-education (intentionally researching about a particular subject), or enrolling for postgraduate courses in your area of calling. The more you equip yourself with knowledge, the more useful you become in solving the problems of our world.

d) Self-evaluation

Not being blind to my weaknesses, I learnt to put in place a character-development system for myself - where I picked on a virtue and concentrated on it for a week, praying, reading and listening to teachings about it, and deliberately using every opportunity that came my way to practice it. When you set your mind on this kind of project, believe me, situations will present themselves that require you to put in practice what you are learning. It is amazing! I did this for the next four years to ensure that these values became part of me. Similarly, you can make a list of the qualities that you admire in other people and work to develop them in your own life too. My quarterly schedule looked like this:

Week	Virtues to reflect on, study and deliberately practice
Week 1	Be patient, persevere
Week 2	Do not envy
Week 3	Don't be self-seeking, demanding your own way
Week 4	Don't be boastful or proud
Week 5	Don't be easily angered
Week 6	Keep no record of wrongs
Week 7	Do not delight in evil but rejoice with the truth
Week 8	Don't be rude
Week 9	Be kind
Week 10	Protect
Week 11	Always trust
Week 12	Always hope

Although I am still a work-in-progress, I can confidently say that I am not who I used to be. As an example, here is a prayer that I noted in my 2014 diary, which I made during a particular Week 5:

"Jesus, I confess my anger and unloving behaviour. Help me to get rid of my personal and petty anger and to love people instead. Help me to forgive and be patient with people, even when they've wronged me. Help me to really love like you love me. I am sorry for all the hurt I've caused through sinful anger. Thank you for dying on the cross for this and other sins.

I confess and repent of the sin of anger today. I trust in you Jesus for my forgiveness and salvation. Please work in my life to make me a loving person. Amen"

I would like to note here, that it is advisable to seek professional help from psychotherapists or counsellors because when you are sick, guess where you go? To the doctor, isn't it? I know that some religious circles believe in prayer alone to solve each and every problem and discourage members from seeking help from professionals. I like the way Dr Sunday Adelaja at one time posed a question to such believers, *"I don't think we are still in the Stone Age, are we?"*

e) Changing the environment

As popularly known, fifty percent of any success in life is based on the environment because it is our environment that moulds us. I deliberately started creating my desired environment as follows:

- Listening to messages and reading books that built me up, not those that birth fear and anger. I am very selective about what I watch too. There are some preachers, places or churches that are a no-go area for me.

    "Not everyone who says to me, 'Lord, Lord,' shall enter the kingdom of heaven, but he who does the will of My Father in heaven."
    Matthew 7:21 NKJV

- I had to edit my friends and contacts lists. If your parents, relatives or friends are not supportive or do not believe in you, then just love them but give them less of your time, or part ways. It is okay.
- Solitude became a monthly affair for me - where I would set aside three days each month just to

be alone - no phone calls, no visitors, no emails, no going out and no cooking! This is an attempt to create space to be still, free from distractions and to build myself up through reading books, listening to messages, working on some project in line with my calling and to fellowship with the 'Author' of my life - the one who knew me before my parents met.

> ***"Before I formed you in the***
> ***womb I knew you."***
> – Jeremiah 1:5 (NKJV)

My friends, run for your dear life if:

i. your church, work-place or home are not developing you into who you are supposed to be
ii. you have no 'voice' in that place
iii. you feel suppressed and oppressed
iv. you are tolerated and not celebrated
v. you are not growing in any way

f) Do good to others and become more sociable

I was previously not a social-media person, but became active on Facebook at the beginning of 2016 and by September I had reached the set limit of friends. My main goal is to reach out to people with words of encouragement and share useful information to help them in life's battles. When we learn to maximise the technology of our day and to connect with people, we build bridges, expand our scope of influence and thereby fight loneliness. We become interesting people to others when we carry the spirit of optimism. We are kind to others through little things like a smile, hug, a gift, or just showing love.

g) Developing a 'thick skin'

I have learnt to remain 'immune' to people's opinions; after all it is my life and not theirs. My friend, you need to realise that not everybody will ever understand or like you and you can never please them all – this is a fact of life! If one door closes, another one will be opened, so don't be afraid of letting people walk out of your life. Out of the billion people on planet earth, some genuine friends will come your way.

Another way to develop the much needed thick skin is when we learn to subdue shame and fear, which always drown us. Do not shy away from sharing your story to others. Someone out there is waiting for it in order to make a positive move. So help them. There are many people who previously struggle with prostitution, drug-addiction, smoking, etc. and are now helping others to overcome the same. The world needs your story, both positive and negative. This is the universal love in action. Through truth and love, we can overcome any situation. When we pay the price to know God's love, so that we can totally learn to live boldly in Him, then external attacks of any form become insignificant.

h) Discovering your self-worth

Many times we look good and seem to have all things together, but actually we are struggling with low self-esteem. It took me time to soak myself into the right teachings of life (mostly by Dr Sunday Adelaja, found at: http://sundayadelajablog.com/) and to discover that I am:

- an image of God
- beloved of God
- born of God
- an authority on the earth
- a carrier of God; He lives in me!

If I really walked with this mind-set and understanding, tell me which 'demon' will be comfortable around me? Which situation can be bigger than my God? Which person can enslave me? Which problem can't I solve?

Another area in which to develop self-worth is in our relationships. Don't hold on to people. You can have friends, but you cannot retain friends by force. If people want to leave you, it's a sign of blessing; let them go! It is the lack of self-esteem, dependency on people or fear of loneliness that forces many women to be beggarly and victims of abuse. Dear lady, learn to respect yourself and know that you are self-sufficient in God.

> **"...Singles, too, must see the penultimate status of marriage. If single Christians don't develop a deeply fulfilling love relationship with Jesus, they will put too much pressure on their DREAM of marriage, and that will create pathology in their lives as well."**
> - Timothy J. Keller

i) Thinking self-dependency and maturity

This is an area I have worked on, am still working on and will continue to work on! The time given to us while still single should be used to build our self-dependency and management concerning our emotions, decisions, time, finances and other areas of life. This helps us not to become victims of emotional and financial dependency on other people. Although, marriage is a union between two mature people, the fact that you are physically mature does not necessarily mean you are mature enough for marriage. Before marriage, we need to be whole and emotionally healthy on our own so as to be fit enough to help and support another person. We cannot give what we do not have. Therefore, my advice for anyone is to seek help to get healing from any wounds from childhood, past relationships or anything you suffered by the hands of so-called deliverance ministers, etc. and become emotionally, psychologically and mentally healthy and mature.

I had to take a deliberate step out of my past into my present; this means a paradigm shift. It is wise to take independent decisions by weighing them and thinking critically and analytically. Argue out your case. Yes, you can ask other people for advice but, at the end of the day make your own decisions without waiting for approval from pastors, parents, prophets, etc. Think self-dependency and maturity. Reading related books and listening to good teachers can be helpful.

j) Focusing on principles rather than societal expectations

Make God your source, not men. Crush that biological clock and put up the God-and-Purpose clock! Hold your head high and own your life and destiny. Remember that your joy and life is dependent on your goals and purpose. Run your life based on the idealistic worldview which includes values like responsibility, contentment, love, truth, faithfulness, integrity, hard work, excellence, focus, perseverance and delayed gratification.

> *"But if as you read this book you're saying to yourself: 'I'd rather be miserably married than be alone.' Well young lady, take out your clown shoes and buckle your seat belt - it's going to be a very bumpy one-woman circus."*
> - Osayi Emokpae Lasisi

As we close up this chapter, here is a report my mother shared with me recently when she met some of my mentees:

> *"These men told me that you are doing a great work in Jinja, that you*

> **are so committed and intelligent. One of them said that he never believed women could be that brilliant; he never respected women before. He said, "Esther is like a man!"**

When we discover ourselves, we correct the wrong mindsets formed in people by the society. But if we don't, then men will continue to think that our purpose is limited to the kitchen, living room and the bedroom! For those of you from an African background, you will relate with this better. If we do not prove our worth, then we consent to the prevailing views about women. When we do not pursue our purpose, society and men in particular will continue to abuse women. So even if you are already married, do not get lost. Discover your purpose and pursue it without any excuse. Your purpose in life should not get lost under your husband's calling; both of you are helpmates to each other in your individual callings – yes the term *individual* is key here because you were an individual before you two met and still remain an individual in the marriage and even in eternity.

Character Aroma Nuggets Part 7:

1) *"Find your inner expression and bless the world with your existence."* - Success Olayemi Fakolade
2) Be your own person, otherwise another person will come to put you in their own 'prison'.
3) *"A season of loneliness and isolation is when the caterpillar gets its wings. Remember that next time you feel alone."* - Mandy Hale, The Single Woman: Life, Love, and a Dash of Sass
4) Be more intentional in all that you do, e.g. in your reading, watching television, going to the library, in the way you dress, meet other people or go to a church service. Be goal-oriented all the time.
5) *"50% of those who are married today are not really supposed to be married! They never prepared themselves and are doing more harm!"* – Dr. Suday Adelaja
6) Being married or having children does not mean that one is living an effective life – drop all those stereotypes and traditions of our world.
7) *"The fastest way to learn is to copy! By copying the people you admire, you are standing on their shoulders, to see further."* – Dr. Sunday Adelaja
8) When you are bitter and angry, you are blinded from seeing the goodness of God in your life. This state weakens your body and can put you at risk of various illnesses.
9) It is much easier to raise a family and bring joy to others when you have discovered your own calling and mission in life.
10) *"If your relationship is draining your energy, making you lose yourself and taking your attention away from God, then you are not in a relationship but a cult. You are busy creating an idol (mini-God) for yourself."* - Kemi Sogunle

Recall and Deliberate (Part 7)

<u>To the General Reader</u>

a) Does the fact that you are physically mature necessarily mean you are mature enough for marriage? If your answer is in the negative, then why do we pressurize singles to get married?
b) Many times we look good and seem to have all things together, but actually we are struggling with low self-esteem. Are you in that relationship or marriage just to boost your morale or public self-esteem?
c) In what ways can we help late singles develop a much needed thick skin especially when it comes to subduing shame and fear which always drowns them?
d) How aware are you of your weaknesses, and what systems are you putting in place to curb them?
e) Having understood that fifty percent of any success in life is based on the environment because it is our environment that moulds us, what kind of environment can you create for yourself and other singles to ensure success?

<u>To the Stigmatized Single Lady</u>

Another area in which to develop self-worth is in your relationships. Don't hold on to people. You can have friends, but you cannot retain friends by force. If people want to leave you, it's a sign of blessing; let them go! It is the lack of self-esteem, dependency on people or fear of loneliness that forces many women to be beggarly and victims of abuse. Dear lady, learn to respect yourself and know that you are self-sufficient in God.

Chapter 8

Learning to Let go and Finding Fulfilment While Single

The Seemingly Hardest Decision, but the Most Liberating

> *"If you are not willing to let anything go, it becomes an idol, a misplaced priority."*
> Dr. Sunday Adelaja

Having looked at self-discovery in the previous chapter, we now need to take steps to allow the new found person to fully emerge and run the race set before them without hindrance. I now present our last chapter with great pleasure because it is the truths shared here that catapulted me to where I am today – a confident, strong and fulfilled lady. I hope that in this chapter, you will find the wisdom needed to thrive and be a winner in life, becoming who you are meant to be and achieving your destiny.

> *"A busy, vibrant, goal-oriented woman is so much more attractive than a woman who waits around for a man to validate her existence."*
> - Mandy Hale

If only we all understood God and His ways, we would avoid most of the burdens and sorrows that we allow into our lives. Learning to let go brings health and life to our bodies. This can only be achieved by accepting one's situation, in this case, singleness, as a blessing from God. He wants to deliver us from the illusions that we, our cultures and our societies have put upon us. God wants to open our eyes to reality, to see as He sees, think like He thinks. Let us now look at some keys to finding fulfilment in life as an unmarried person:

1. The process of letting go

In November 2015, I attended a History Makers Training course in Ukraine organised by Dr. Sunday Adelaja. One of the exercises we had to do totally revolutionised my life – it pushed me to live for God alone and for his purposes. I knew then that if I never got married, it wasn't going to be an issue and that I would remain happy in God, focusing on my assignment on earth; and if I ever got married, then good too, because that would be an opportunity for me to grow in different aspects of life. I became very comfortable with both scenarios and was at peace with myself.

> **"Get the thought or question of marriage out of your mind. Let that question be God's, not your own headache, set your mind free!"**
>
> **"Anything that is for you will always find you. It's not your own business to hunt for them."**
>
> **"When you have convinced heaven that God is your number one, then all things work out for your good."**
> - Dr. Sunday Adelaja

In that exercise, we were told to analyse ourselves and come up with a list of fifteen to twenty most important things in our lives that are taking up all our focus, those things that we were living for, praying for or aspiring to attain. Then we were required at several stages to keep cancelling things as a sign of letting go until we were left with only one item on the list! We realised that one thing is the most valuable in our individual lives. This was no joke my friends, but a solemn and sacred moment. There were tears of pain as an internal battle with myself and with my Creator God was going on!

> *"There are some places in life where you can only go alone. Embrace the beauty of your solo journey."*
> - Mandy Hale

For illustration purposes, here is how my list dropped from fifteen to one and that *number one* truly became my only 'gold' in life:

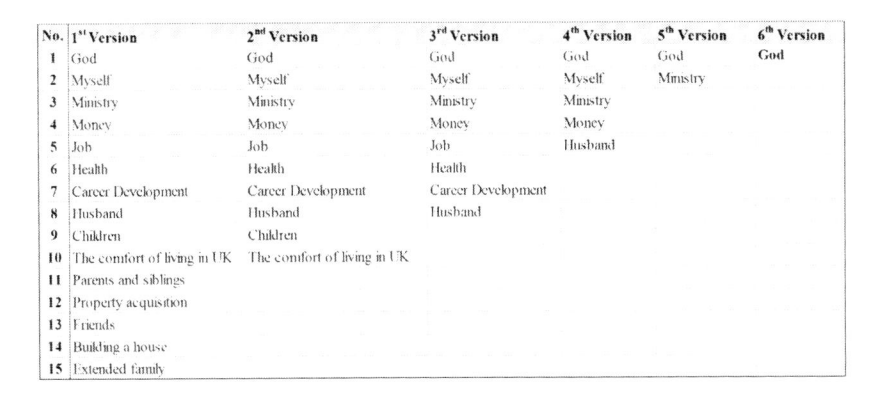

No.	1st Version	2nd Version	3rd Version	4th Version	5th Version	6th Version
1	God	God	God	God	God	God
2	Myself	Myself	Myself	Myself	Ministry	
3	Ministry	Ministry	Ministry	Ministry		
4	Money	Money	Money	Money		
5	Job	Job	Job	Husband		
6	Health	Health	Health			
7	Career Development	Career Development	Career Development			
8	Husband	Husband	Husband			
9	Children	Children				
10	The comfort of living in UK	The comfort of living in UK				
11	Parents and siblings					
12	Property acquisition					
13	Friends					
14	Building a house					
15	Extended family					

> *"I had struggled so hard and so long that I had simply exhausted myself, only to find that God had all the time in the world to wait for me to allow Him to free me."*
> - Michelle McKinney Hammond

I need to stress here that sacrificing all other things on your list does not necessarily mean that you will never have them! Jesus Christ said, *"For whoever desires to save his life will lose it, but whoever loses his life for my sake will find it."* Matthew 16: 25 (NKJV)

This was an exercise that helped me to realise my priorities in life and to know who I am living to please. When I started walking in this understanding, I began to experience fulfilment and God has given me a 'gift' I thought I would never have – a handsome man as my fiancé! God knows the desires of our hearts and will provide the help we need in life, be encouraged always by this truth.

2. Connect to your Source

The first step is to go to God to regain your calmness and to come out of your 'panic' zone. It is in this state of peace with God and in God, that we are able to find solutions. We are encouraged to go on a journey with God through a regular practice of solitude, without distractions.

> **"Now acquaint yourself with Him, and be at peace; thereby good will come to you."**
> - Job 22:21 (NKJV)

Trust and hide in God – by doing so, all the worldly things begin to diminish before our eyes. We then begin to grow in God's assurance and love. When we regularly fellowship with our Maker, the owner of our lives, the one who knows all things, He comforts us and we re-gain confidence in ourselves.

> **"Be anxious for nothing, but in everything by prayer and supplication, with thanksgiving, let your requests be made known to God; and the peace of God, which surpasses all understanding, will guard your hearts and minds through Christ Jesus."**
> - Philippians 4:6-7 (NKJV)

3. Physical things are temporary

Stop relying on the temporary things of this world. God is our pillar and our only hope not people, ministry, wealth, jobs, money, friends, family, children, spouse, etc. Come to think of it, we too are just temporal on the earth so nothing is dependable except God who dwells in eternity and who is our destination. We need to separate ourselves from those things that take the place of God in our lives; our desire to please Him must be supreme in our lives. Full stop!

> ***"Let us crush these so-called biological clocks that give us nothing but fear and encourage us to make stupid decisions. Let us crush these biological clocks that hurt us and rob us of the fabulous lives that Jesus died to give us. These clocks not only hurt us but hurt many generations after us."***
> *- Osayi Emokpae Lasisi*

4. Focusing on your calling

We do not remember people because they have got married and had children. Marriage is a beautiful thing, don't get me wrong, but the great names we hear about are those people who maximised their potential in innovations and inventions, who touched lives by removing shame, wiping tears and lifting others to a better life.

> ***"When you feel pain and love for a particular problem or need in the society, or a particular place or people, this may be pointing to your destiny. Your promise land is where your passion lies. It is where your heart quickens, where you feel an almost supernatural hunger to intervene and improve a situation."***[40]
> *– Dr Sunday Adelaja*

The best way to overcome the battles of the single life is to be focused on your calling, being a blessing to others and freeing yourself from people's expectations. There is no marriage in heaven, and all we shall receive is the reward of our faithfulness to God and His assignment for our lives. A book that can help you get more understanding on calling is: '*Who Am I? Why Am I here? How to discover your purpose and calling in life.*' by Sunday Adelaja. I can testify to the fact that once we are sold out to God's agenda, we become happier people. Oh yes! You can find so much joy and fulfilment that you forget your marital status. I usually remember that I am single when I'm invited to a wedding. When my fiancé and I met, I was not thinking of marriage at all, but was too busy with my calling and self-development. It was a surprise! God will send the 'helpmate' you need at the right time, when you least expect it.

> **"One of the greatest advantages of singleness is the potential for greater focus on Christ and accomplishing work for Him."**
> - Elizabeth George

God tries to get us to the place where we pursue Him and His purpose and not our own. We were created for Him and for His pleasure.

> **"For by Him all things were created that are in heaven and that are on earth, visible and invisible, whether thrones or dominions or principalities or powers. All things were created through Him and for Him."**
> - Colossians 1:16 (NKJV)

This deals with the priority of embracing Kingdom principles to become Christ-like in character, motivation, attitude, action or lifestyle. The life pursuit of every believer individually, and every church corporately, should be focused on extending the culture or values and principles of the kingdom of God on earth.

> *"But seek first the kingdom of God and His righteousness, and all these things shall be added to you."*
> Matthew 6:33 (NKJV)

5. Have the moral courage

Moral courage is needed for you not to compromise the values and the principles governing your life. There are great rewards in this. Moral courage is needed in understanding that every one of our experiences, either negative or positive, is a blessing and should be shared to help others. You need to overcome shame and put a high price on the lives that would benefit from your story. There are a variety of tools that one could use, for example, writing books, posting messages and video clips on social media, blogging, etc. In doing so, you are turning your 'pain' into a 'gain' for yourself and for others too.

> *"I define myself... Make peace with what you have... Make the best of it... You really learn to enjoy yourself."*
> - Zoe Saldana

6. Continuous self-development

Always convert your time into the development of new skills, acquire the ability to work hard, overcome laziness and idleness! Gain the ability to be organised and be self-disciplined, which makes you a winner. After sometime, you stop pitying yourself because you have chosen to accept God's blessing.

Another skill to develop is leadership – the capacity to influence others positively. We all have this seed, but it needs to be nurtured. Remember that character, the self-imposed discipline, is the foundation of true leadership.

7. Valuing time

There are so many distractions that can demand our attention and time: friends and colleagues, church activities, parties, TV, family, housework, cooking, shopping, holidays, gardening, cleaning, etc. But if we have set goals, then we have to divert all our energy and attention towards these by learning to 'fight' for every minute of our life. We need to set boundaries in our lives – it's not every wedding that you need to attend, it's not every meeting where your presence is required, and it's not every person that cannot do without your handshake! Free yourself from the pressures of people-pleasing and learn to say "No" without feeling guilty about it. After all, it won't kill anyone! We can also get external help to delegate some tasks to others so that we can use more time for something that pushes us towards our goals. By being more strategic and organised in all we do, we become a master of life, not a slave!

I do hope, dear reader, that the above mentioned principles have energised you to pursue your dreams or calling with all your heart. Enough is enough of excuses for not living a fulfilled life and being single is definitely not one of them. See you at the top!

Character Aroma Nuggets Part 8:

1) Don't be 'religious', be practical – grow in all aspects e.g. wisdom, character.
2) Your mood, joy, peace, must depend on what is inside of you and not on external circumstances.
3) Base your decision on facts and proof, not words. Words are cheap!
4) Don't allow anyone to tell you that you cannot do something because of your marital status. Lift your head high, and walk away to prove them wrong.
5) Live at peace with yourself by refusing to allow any form of mental torture just because people do not understand you. They don't have to!
6) *"If I don't understand the actions and reactions of other people, it is my problem. I should resolve it myself. If anybody does not understand me, it is their problem, they should resolve it themselves."* – Dr. Sunday Adelaja
7) The first weapon of our warfare is truth. Satan dominates through deception, lies, ignorance. *"But those who know the truth shall be strong and will do exploits."* - Daniel 11:32
8) Be strategic - work on the factors of success: Knowledge (ten percent), Character (forty percent), and Environment (fifty percent).
9) Never leave your destiny in the hands of other men, circumstances or God! Don't wait on God, be busy pursuing your purpose and God will meet you there.
10) Plan for your life, write down your goals for ten, twenty, fifty years ahead. Be passionate about them.

Recall and Deliberate (Part 8)

<u>To the General Reader</u>

I hope by now you must have understood the perspective at which I am coming from and what must be done to combat this malady. But you see, it cannot only be done through this book. It is our collective duty to stamp out a value or culture that does not work for people's good or that demeans any human being. It is time to rise up and be up and doing. It is time to practice all the ideas that have been put forward by writing this book and then our world can be a better place for us all to live. I hope I will receive testimonies of how this book has brought transformation to your life and those around you soon. Thanks.

<u>To the Stigmatized Single Lady</u>

I hope by now you must have seen yourself as God sees you. To say anything less is a deception. However, there are areas you might need personally to work on in your life. Pay attention to developing yourself continuously as well as turning your weaknesses into strengths. There is a gift God has placed in everyone's hands and that is time! Always convert your time into the development of new skills, acquire the ability to work hard, overcome laziness and idleness! Gain the ability to be organised and be self-disciplined, which makes you a winner. After sometime, you stop pitying yourself because you have chosen to accept God's blessing.

Conclusion

The Power of Thriving and Shining is in
Your Mind and Hands; Use It!

"We have the duty of formulating, of summarising, and of communicating our conclusions, in intelligible form, in recognition of the right of other free minds to utilise them in making their own decisions."
Ronald fisher

In this book, we have explored what it feels like to be single in our day. The aim of the different stories and citations was to let you the readers know the reality of the stigmatisation and the problem of stereotyping. We discovered how influential the home environment can be on the mindset of a child, affecting their view on marriage, their future decisions and behaviour patterns. We can now agree that culture, societal expectations, religiosity and wrong doctrines have caused a significant level of damage to the lives of unmarried women in one way or the other in most societies especially Africa.

Facing the brutal facts helped us understand why there are many unmarried people in our societies today. I then gave you forty examples of influential people to prove the fact that being single cannot stop anyone from becoming a great achiever in life. Throughout the book, the emphasis has been not to play the blame game but to take some drastic actions to show that we are responsible for our own lives and happiness. Looking at self-discovery helped us to get to know our real core, the genesis of our greatness. Then we looked at principles to help us learn the art of letting go of those things that we previously held onto so dearly, in order to fulfil our destinies.

When you look around you, do you notice single women or mothers? Have you tried to find out how they are coping? Do they look happy and fulfilled? If not, have a chat with them about what you have learned or better still, get them this book. It is good to look out for one another. In doing so, you have become a channel of blessing to others and this alone is so rewarding.

Let us try to always speak out when we see things that are not right. We cannot change any society by keeping silent or remaining indifferent. We should be a 'voice' for the voiceless. This is why I decided to write this book – to fight the stigma against single women. I encourage you, dear reader, to join me in this fight and so something. It could be to start holding seminars to talk about these things or offering counsel to those who are struggling. Get in touch with me and I will offer some guidance in this area.

We must say 'good-bye' to the things that have held us bound for years and embrace the liberty that biblical principles offer. There is true fulfilment when we align ourselves with how God our creator, intended for us to live. This power is within us, we just need to tap into it and put it in use.

I would like to encourage you to continue to reflect on the principles shared in this book, review the assignments and make strategies and plans for the life you want to have. Remember my friend, that marriage is not an end in itself. It is not meant for everybody, especially those that are not well prepared for it. Such people are the cause of most, if not, all of the heartaches in our world today. Please, do not become part of these statistics.

To make our world better, we need to make our own contribution through adequate preparation, and our 'gifts', as I have testified, will come to us by all means. And even if it does not happen, you are still not alone – you are already a 'bride' of Christ! Be so engrossed in your calling and vision that you forget about your marital status. This is indeed the richest and most fulfilling life!

Run your race, if God brings the right person into your life, fantastic – that is a bonus! Embrace His gift to you. If this never happens, perfect! The gift of singleness that you have is priceless! Embrace it with all your heart, never look back. Live your life happily and for God's glory. Help me to spread the word so that many more single ladies are liberated. Let us pass on the principles learned to the young people, let us raise up a new generation that understands the true meaning and purpose of life, and our world shall indeed be a better place.

If you are a single lady, I hope that this book has greatly boosted your faith and self-esteem. So keep smiling and loving! May we all become fruitful for the kingdom of God. It is those 'fruits' that we shall present before our Creator at the end of our earthly journey. It is my prayer that you will live a life of love, truth, integrity, diligence and responsibility.

We read about many world legendary leaders like Mother Theresa, William Wilberforce, Martin Luther King Junior, Nelson Mandela, and the list goes on and on. These brave people fought one form of injustice or the other. They chose not to be indifferent. What about you? What can you do? You could start by being a 'faith' general of your own life first, before reaching out to others. If you are a single woman, please grow your faith to be strong enough, to cause a positive transformation in your own life. See what these faith generals did:

> *"And what more shall I say? For the time would fail me to tell of Gideon and Barak and Samson and Jephthah, also of David and Samuel and the prophets: who through faith subdued kingdoms, worked righteousness, obtained promises, stopped the mouths of lions, quenched the violence of fire, escaped the edge of the sword, out of weakness were made strong, became valiant in battle, turned to flight the armies of the aliens."*
> Hebrews 11:32-34 (NKJV)

Oh yes, single ladies! Let us arise and silence the negativity around us, beat the status-quo, adopt positive life-governing values, be role models, and influence the world for God. Let our goal be to please the Master and make Him proud of us, to say:

> *"Well done, good and faithful servant; you were faithful over a few things, I will make you ruler over many things. Enter into the joy of your Lord."*
> Matthew 25:21 (NKJV)

If this book has been a blessing to you, please contact me on kues09@yahoo.com. I would love to hear from you. It would also be helpful if you left your review on Amazon or on our Overcoming Stigmatisation Facebook page: https://www.facebook.com/CAPTransformationAgents/

All proceeds from the sale of this book will be used to support the charitable work of *Character Aroma Project*. For more details visit: www.characteraromaproject.org

Many thanks for your support.

End Notes

* Names with an asterisk are pseudonyms.

Chapter 3

1. http://www.our-africa.org/women - viewed on 14/12/2016
2. http://www.our-africa.org/senegal/fighting-for-her-children - viewed on 14/12/2016
3. http://www.bbc.co.uk/news/world-africa-37659863 - viewed 14/10/2016
4. http://www.thehookmag.com/2016/10/heres-average-age-people-lose-virginity-around-world-109529/ - viewed on 14/12/2015
5. http://www.worldatlas.com/articles/countries-with-the-lowest-mother-s-mean-age-at-first-birth.html - viewed on 14/12/2016
6. http://sundayadelajablog.com/want-rich-husband-rich-wife-2/ - viewed on 14/12/2016
7. http://thoughtcatalog.com/kim-quindlen/2015/01/17-reasons-we-constantly-feel-pressured-to-get-engaged-before-were-ready/ - viewed on 15/12/2016
8. http://www.idiva.com/news-relationships/how-to-resist-the-pressure-to-get-married/23102 - viewed on 16/12/2016

Chapter 4

9. http://smu-facweb.smu.ca/~wmills/course322/16African_Churches.html - viewed on 17/12/2016
10. http://sundayadelajablog.com/leave-us-alone-every-mmm-participant-already-lost-article-7/ viewed on 20/12/2016

Chapter 5

11. http://edition.cnn.com/2010/LIVING/08/19/single.in.america/ as viewed on 27/11/2016
12. http://www.gallup.com/poll/6961/what-percentage-population-gay.aspx viewed on 25/12/2016
13. http://www.dailymail.co.uk/news/article-3210826/Proof-eligible-man-shortage-four-college-educated-women-three-males-don-t-think-trying-one-Manhattan.html viewed 22/12/2016.
14. http://www.psychalive.org/why-am-i-still-single/ viewed on 20/12/2016. Article: Why Am I Still Single? 8 Reasons People Often Stay Single, by Dr. Lisa Firestone is the Director of Research and Education at The Glendon Association.

Chapter 6

15. http://www.goodreads.com/quotes/37285-i-love-a-tree-more-than-a-man viewed on 28/12/2016
16. http://quotegeek.com/literature/jane-austen/6011/ viewed on 27/12/2016
17. http://quotes.lifehack.org/quote/henry-david-thoreau/i-have-never-found-a-companion-that/ viewed on 28/12/2016
18. The Woman's Column, August 14, 1897, quoted in Sherr, p. 13
19. Gordon, Ann (2000). The Selected Papers of Elizabeth Cady Stanton and Susan B. Anthony. p. 41

20. Harper, Ida (1898–1908). The Life and Work of Susan B. Anthony. Vol. 2, p. 516
21. Blackwell, Elizabeth (1895). Pioneer Work in Opening the Medical Profession to Women: Autobiographical Sketches. London and New York: Longmans, Green, and Co. Retrieved 17 July 2016.
22. Cullen-DuPont, Kathryn (August 1, 2000). Encyclopedia of women's history in America. Infobase Publishing. pp. 8–9. ISBN 978-0-8160-4100-8. Retrieved November 28, 2011.
23. http://www.azquotes.com/quote/524893 viewed on 28/12/2016
24. Laplante, Phillip A. (1999). Comprehensive Dictionary of Electrical Engineering 1999. Springer. p. 635. ISBN 9783540648352.
25. https://www.brainyquote.com/quotes/quotes/n/nikolatesl127569.html viewed on 28/12/2016
26. Steinhauer, Harry (Autumn 1983). "Franz Kafka: A World Built on a Lie". The Antioch Review. Yellow Springs, Ohio. 41 (4): 390. Doi: 10.2307/4611280. JSTOR 4611280.
27. https://www.goodreads.com/author/quotes/546818.Greta_Garbo viewed on 28/12/2016
28. http://www.biographyonline.net/nobelprize/mother_teresa.html
29. "President Bush Honours Medal of Freedom Recipients" (Press release). The White House. November 5, 2007.
30. http://www.huffingtonpost.com/samara-oshea/ten-tremendous-women-who_b_332697.html
31. http://www.womenshealthmag.com/sex-and-love/famous-quotes-single-ladies
32. http://www.hellomagazine.com/film/2013111515661/oprah-winfrey-talks-marriage-lorraine-kelly/ viewed on 28/12/2016
33. http://www.more.com/love-sex/single-life/10-single-women-who-redefined-spinsterhood/susan-boyle

Esther Kuganja

34. "Kristin Davis." www.oxfam.org. Oxfam International. Retrieved 19 October 2016.
35. http://www.popsugar.com/celebrity/photo-gallery/34508082/image/34508309/Kristin-Davis viewed on 29/12/2016
36. http://www.nextleadership.org/about-us/ viewed on 29/12/2016
37. Kathy Griffin (2012). *The 100 Most Influential People in the World*: Chelsea Handler. Time Magazine. April 18, 2012.
38. http://www.nydailynews.com/entertainment/gossip/chelsea-handler-dishes-romance-andre-balazs-not-marriage-material-article-1.1065782 viewed on 28/12/2016
39. http://www.eonline.com/de/news/545985/charlize-theron-is-happily-unmarried-at-38-a-life-is-good-if-it-s-the-life-that-you-want

Chapter 8

40. Adelaja, Sunday (2017). Ways to identify your promised land. Article viewed at: http://sundayadelajablog.com/wednesdays-nuggets-pastor-sunday-31/ on 11/01/2017

Bibliography

1) Adelaja, Sunday (2009). *Time is Life. History Makers Honour time.* Favour House, Ukraine.
2) Adelaja, Sunday. (2016). *Who Am I? Why Am I Here? – How to discover your purpose and calling in Life.* Golden Pen Limited, Milton Keynes, United Kingdom.
3) Bien, Sufficient (2016). *If You Want a Rich Husband, Be a Rich Wife.* 21/09/2016, viewed at: http://sundayadelajablog.com/want-rich-husband-rich-wife-2/ on 18/10/2016
4) Birger Jon (2015). Date-onomics: How Dating Became a Lopsided Numbers Game. Workman Publishing.
5) Blackwell, Elizabeth (1895). *Pioneer Work in Opening the Medical Profession to Women*: Autobiographical Sketches. London and New York: Longmans, Green, and Co. Retrieved 17 July 2016. https://en.wikipedia.org/wiki/Elizabeth_Blackwell
6) Cloud Henry, Townsend John (1992). *Boundaries: When to say yes, how to say no to take control of your life.* Zondervan.
7) Coleman, Kate (2010). *7 Deadly Sins of Women in Leadership. Overcoming self-defeating behaviour in work & ministry.* Next Leadership.
8) Hale, Mandy (2013). *The Single Woman: Life, Love, and a Dash of Sass.* Thomas Nelson, Inc.
9) https://en.wikipedia.org

10) Keller Timothy and Keller Kathy (2011). The Meaning of Marriage: Facing the Complexities of Commitment with the Wisdom of God. Hodder & Stoughton Ltd, London.
11) Okome, O. (2003) 'What Women, Whose Development.' African Women and Feminism: Reflecting on the Politics of Sisterhood. Trenton: Africa World Press.
12) Osar-Emokpae, Osayi (2011). *Impossible Is Stupid. 57 truths to help you beat loneliness and depression and live the fabulous life you always wanted.* CreateSpace Independent Publishing Platform.
13) Quitmeyer, Maitland (2015). *31 Famous Unmarried People Who Prove That Being Single Is Badass* – posted on Feb 8, 2015, viewed 20/11/2016 at: https://www.buzzfeed.com/maitlandquitmeyer/this-list-of-31-famous-people-who-never-married-will-inspire?utm_term=.oo883ro3E#.buy958W5N
14) Sufficient, Bien. (2016). Why Purpose Is Greater Than Marriage. 21/09/2016, viewed at: http://sundayadelajablog.com/purpose-greater-marriage/ on 18/10/2016

Other Services by the Author

Esther is the founder of *Character Aroma Project* (CAP), a non-governmental Organisation (NGO) currently registered in Uganda. The main aim of this charity is to transform Ugandan life through character-building and development. We hope this will create a culture of discipline in Uganda and result in tremendous benefits like happier homes, purposeful youths, responsible parents, a good reputation for Uganda on the international platform and thereby attracting more foreign investors and much more.

CAP's Vision:

'Uganda, the byword for character'.

Mission Statement:

'To improve, strengthen and increase the quality of Ugandan life through character building'.

Goals:

1. To raise leaders of character who will take responsibility for their nation and the world;
2. To establish a culture of discipline in Uganda through trainings, seminars and workshops;

3. To demonstrate overtime, a marked improvement in the character and culture of discipline of the people of Uganda;
4. To educate the population against corruption and discrimination.
5. To partner with schools and bring the elements of character development into the education system.
6. Enhance Uganda's reputation in terms of justice and righteousness on the International platform
7. Raise the standards of customer service year on year for each of the next 10 years
8. Reduce Uganda's bribery prevalence rate by at least 50% in the next 20 years.

CAP Core Values (RID):

- Responsibility
- Integrity
- Diligence

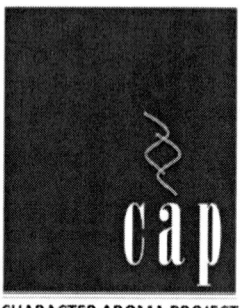

We aim at producing leaders who are responsible citizens of integrity and are diligent at continuous personal-development.

CHARACTER AROMA PROJECT

About the Author

Esther Kuganja is founder and Executive director of Character Aroma Project, a Non-governmental Organisation whose mission is to improve, strengthen and increase the quality of life in Uganda through character building. Her main interests are leadership development and national transformation.

Esther's passion is to raise leaders who can take responsibilities for their families, communities and nation. She has broad work experience in Data Analytics, Lecturing, Administration and management. One of her favourite quotes is: *'Life is not measured by its duration, but by its contribution."* Dr. Myles Munroe. Esther's extracurricular activities include singing, listening to music, reading, movies and travelling.

Having been single and a virgin at the age of forty, Esther has had a rich experience and has been a stereotyped victim herself and wanted to leave the pearls of wisdom that she picked up along her journey to help others not only the unmarried ladies of today and to pass on the same to generations to come.

Esther Kuganja

Contact details of the Author

Blog: http://character-aroma-project.tumblr.com
Email: kues09@yahoo.com
Facebook: http://facebook.com/EstherKuganjaCAP
Phone: +447960851754
Twitter: https://twitter.com/characteraroma
Website: http://www.characteraromaproject.org

Lightning Source UK Ltd.
Milton Keynes UK
UKOW08f1515230517
301827UK00001B/185/P